La Rive

La Rive

The taste of the Amstel

Edwin Kats
Alma Huisken

Photography: Bart Van Leuven

STICHTING KUNSTBOEK

Preface

In a most appropriate place – at the chef's table in the *La Rive* kitchen – Edwin Kats recently asked me if I would write the preface to his first cookbook. Although I would rather cook than write, I felt honored. So, it is with great pride that I present you this beautiful cookbook.

I first met Edwin Kats in April 1994, when he joined our team at *de Swaen* in Oisterwijk. At the time, *de Swaen* was going through a difficult period. After many demanding years behind the stove, I wanted to spread my wings, but I could hardly combine that with maintaining the high standards in the restaurant. I had to make a choice. A choice made much easier by Edwin's arrival: a new chef was born. Starting as *sous chef* he gradually – and inevitably – took over the reins.

I take great joy from the fact that Edwin found his place in the restaurant of the beautiful Amstel Hotel. I already knew him as an ambitious chef, so it came as no surprise when *La Rive* regained its second Michelin star so shortly after his arrival. When I heard the news, I felt proud and elated.

"A good chef should be a bit opinionated", that is my motto. I still often think back with great joy to the discussions Edwin and I had in the small hours of the morning. With his passion for the business, and his consistent way of reasoning and talking about the trade, he gained my respect. He still possesses a professional attitude and unbridled energy; he knows what is expected of him, and he fully realizes this.

Edwin also understands the art of cooking great classics. His stocks and sauces are powerful because of the time and attention he devotes to them, and his creations of unusual types of meat testify to his craftsmanship. To prepare *abats* (as variety meats are called in our trade) as well as he does, and presenting them – down to the finest detail – in a contemporary way, is truly an achievement of the rarest kind.

I will not soon forget that evening in the kitchen at *La Rive*, where I experienced the pinnacle of gastronomy. Conceptualizing and preparing dishes is very different from properly assembling a book. Both activities should be done with intense effort and great accuracy. We have had the opportunity to sample his culinary achievements; now they are immortalized in this beautiful book, and we can savor them with each reading and rereading.

Congratulations, Edwin, on the realization of this beautiful book that will inspire many people in the trade – and hopefully at home as well – to cook beautifully and inspired!

Cas Spijkers
Oisterwijk, 2003

"Running a kitchen is a question of anticipation: thinking what can go wrong, before it actually happens."

E. Kats

On the shores
of the Amstel

On the shores
of the Amstel

It could not have been more informal. My first meeting with Amstel Inter-Continental Amsterdam Director Christian Beek takes place in a rolling little boat, splashing on the river. Gallantly he helped me to board the *La Reine*, moored to the shore of the Amstel Hotel together with the *Libelle*. While Executive *Chef de Cuisine*, Edwin Kats, and Executive Sous Chef, Dennis Kuipers, were readying themselves to prepare a choice of beautiful dishes, which photographer Bart van Leuven would capture digitally, my curiosity is piqued about this mobile sub-division of the hotel. Sailing on a saloon boat and raising a glass of champagne with a small group of people whilst enjoying lunch or hors d'oeuvres (hot and cold), is merely one of the attractive extras this majestic hotel offers her guests. All this on top op what already appears to be such a special hotel. As Christian Beek says, leaning against *La Reine's* gleaming mahogany: "The Amstel Hotel is large, on her small scale."

Courteous style

It was Robert Kranenborg, a celebrated previous chef, who showed me the golden Hall of Mirrors, a breathtaking space seemingly too beautiful for meetings, rather creating an ambiance redolent of rustling gowns and elegant waltzes. Fortunately, the Amstel Hotel follows the concept 'from boardroom to ballroom'; reaching back to the former function of this majestic space, and dancing does indeed take place. The Hall of Mirrors, the lobby with its stately staircase, the plush carpets and the general atmosphere of these striking premises echo its past grandeur. Since opening its doors in 1867, the Amstel has been one of the grandest and most luxurious hotels in the Netherlands. Immediately engaged by royal and aristocratic guests, the Amstel could not only compete effortlessly with hotels abroad, but appeared to offer more. Here one finds courteous style combined with a personal touch, and even a dash of Amsterdam humor. One would never expect this behind the somewhat stately appearance (including liveried porters).

It could not have been more informal. My first meeting with Amstel Inter-Continental Amsterdam Director Christian Beek takes place in a rolling little boat, splashing on the river. Gallantly he helped me to board the La Reine, moored to the shore of the Amstel Hotel together with the Libelle. While Executive Chef de Cuisine, Edwin Kats, and Executive Sous Chef, Dennis Kuipers, were readying themselves to prepare a choice of beautiful dishes, which photographer Bart van Leuven would capture digitally, my curiosity is piqued about this mobile sub-division of the hotel. Sailing on a saloon boat and raising a glass of champagne with a small group of people whilst enjoying lunch or hors d'oeuvres (hot and cold), is merely one of the attractive extras this majestic hotel offers her guests. All this on top op what already appears to be such a special hotel. As Christian Beek says, leaning against La Reine's gleaming mahogany: "The Amstel Hotel is large, on her small scale".

Courteous style

It was Robert Kranenborg, a celebrated previous chef, who showed me the golden Hall of Mirrors, a breathtaking space seemingly too beautiful for meetings, rather creating an ambiance redolent of rustling gowns and elegant waltzes. Fortunately, the Amstel Hotel follows the concept 'from boardroom to ballroom'; reaching back to the former function of this majestic space, and dancing does indeed take place. The Hall of Mirrors, the lobby with its stately staircase, the plush carpets and the general atmosphere of these striking premises echo its past grandeur. Since opening its doors in 1867, the Amstel has been one of the grandest and most luxurious hotels in the Netherlands. Immediately engaged by royal and aristocratic guests, the Amstel could not only compete effortlesly with hotels abroad, but appeared to offer more. Here one finds courteous style combined with a personal touch, and even a dash of Amsterdam humor. One would never expect this behind the somewhat stately appearance (including liveried porters).

I run into General Manager Christian Beek again, this time in a stylish meeting room. Between two meetings, he grins while biting into a toasted ham and cheese sandwich ("You see, the kitchens can even make this!"). I ask him about the *La Rive's* situation, exceptional because the restaurant is inextricably bound to the hotel. Is there recognition for the restaurant among his hotel guests? Beek: "Yes and no. *La Rive's* image for the foreign market segment – and that's a significant part of our public – still needs some work; for the local market, the restaurant has earned its reputation and we can be sure of attracting a diverse clientele. But many foreign visitors are not used to a hotel restaurant offering more than value for money. After all, a spectacular experience awaits them, and without even having to leave the building! That is truly remarkable: we are also the only hotel in the global Inter-Continental chain – to which the Amstel belongs – with a two-star restaurant."

He carefully weighs his words: "No matter how unique we find the situation, it does not necessarily have a classic relation of cost to turnover. I see it as my job to support the position of *La Rive* in all ways possible; within the hotel, but also within the chain."

A proper balance

Beek (married, with three children) is only 46, but has many years of experience working abroad. His experience, combined with a relaxed attitude, makes this son of Antwerp look and sounds more like a sporting diplomat than a traditional hotel manager. Even in his youth he found himself in an environment with an international touch: Beek attended a Dutch-speaking school, but his home language was French. After his education in Switzerland (in Glion, near Montreux), his career followed the hierarchy of the hotel trade step by step. As Food & Beverage Manager and later Resident Manager, he took part in the management of large hotels in London, Athens and Washington D.C. (the famous *Willard* on Pennsylvania Avenue, where every American president has stayed). For nearly seven years he worked as General Manager at the *American* on the Leidse plein in Amsterdam, before the Amstel called him.

"My strongest attraction to the Amstel is that, despite its size, this establishment appears to be one of the few hotels in the world able to play a significant role in the international arena. The modest size, understandable in its dimensions, will also stay like this: we can never expand the hotel, only improve it and pro-actively adapt to the market and wishes of the modern guest. We remain classic, and offer as much professional distance as the guests wish, but we have left behind the overly formal – perhaps even touching on arrogant – atmosphere that once used to reign here. This is also true for the restaurant's appearance, for that matter. Do not expect any significant changes, but rather subtle adjustments – from the personnel uniforms to *La Rive's* fabrics."

Christian Beek and Edwin Kats joined the Amstel more or less the same time, in mid-2000. Beek recognized a great chef in the young Kats, one able to reach even greater heights. "Kats has an individual vision for the kitchen, and I grant him his freedom in that as much as possible. He is charismatic and has outspoken opinions, but he has also shown himself open to compromise as long as you can offer good arguments. I give him feedback and assist from the sideline, where necessary. Not only regarding the kitchen but also on facilities. If Edwin finds it necessary to acquire new knowledge and inspiration by traveling to Milan to visit a new restaurant, his ticket is ready."

Philosophizing on the categories of chefs, Beek distinguishes between those chefs who may be gifted in the culinary area, but less so in managing a kitchen, and chefs who present the opposite. "What makes Kats remarkable is that he is able to offer both, in the proper balance. He cooks with the best and happens to be a born leader. That is something you don't often find."

The royal history

Before Edwin Kats became Executive Chef three years ago, *La Rive* had already built its reputation with chefs such as John Halvemaan and Robert Kranenborg. A few years ago, under the very same Kranenborg, worked a deputy chef named Edwin Kats. He is quite familiar with the hotel and restaurant. So familiar that he does not shy away from large-scale operations like Christmas (with groups of up to 1,500 people) or a Royal Wedding, for which the Amstel offered accommodation while *La Rive* took care of food and drink.

In the Royal Suite (a home away from home, with an undoubtedly seldom used kitchenette), the hostess showing me around the hotel relives memories of the reception and the special guests with obvious pleasure. "Queen Margarethe of Denmark was late leaving for the ceremony, but she literally came storming down the large staircase with a grin, the ever-present cigarette in her mouth. You don't expect that from a queen, but she said that she really felt at home here."

The strong ties with the Royal House can be seen in no less than four grand happenings: the Amstel played host to the wedding reception of Queen Beatrix and Prince Claus, the 25th wedding anniversary in 1962 of the then Queen Juliana and Prince Bernhard, the celebration of Queen Beatrix's 60th birthday in 1998 and, of course, The Wedding of 2002, that of Prince Willem-Alexander and Princess Máxima.

Gym since 1870

Located on a tranquil part of the Amstel, the elegant hotel originally had 111 rooms which – bearing in mind the modern requirements of space and comfort – were renovated in 1992 to become 79 rooms and suites of varying furnishings and luxury, crowned with one full apartment, the Royal Suite. This consists of an entry hall,

a dining room with seating for eight people and adjoining kitchen, two royal bedrooms with bathrooms and a comfortable lounge. The most luxurious suites boast bathrooms with the famous Amstel showers: measuring nearly one and a half meters in diameter and guaranteeing the ultimate experience in refreshing showers.

Each room comes equipped with the tools of modern communication. If you wish, your favorite CDs and videos could be waiting; the private bar can provide your preferred drinks. Apart from the services you may expect from a hotel of equal stature (like being picked up from the airport, for example), the hotel also has space for a swimming pool (level with the river) and exercise areas. Here, too, the Amstel has a reputation to uphold: as early as 1879 the famous doctor John Metzger introduced gymnastic exercises and massages for hotel guests. His fame reached the aristocracy and royal households of Europe, who visited the hotel partly to make use of his services. Visitors included the Russian czar and czarina and the shah of Persia, later followed by the modern royal families of Spain, Sweden and Britain.

The hotel has housed not only great diplomats and captains of industry, but also scientists and artists (Gustave Eiffel and Henry Moore), alongside stars of stage and screen from the past and present, like Marlène Dietrich, Orson Welles, Audrey Hepburn, Liz Taylor, Jeremy Irons and Steven Spielberg.

The charm of the Amstel

Whether you are a VIP or just coming to have a cup of tea, all mouths are fed and refreshed by a staff of around 35 chefs, who not only see to their manager's ham and cheese sandwich, but also to the breakfast and room service requirements of the hotel guests, the drinks on the terraces, the salon boats and in the conservatory, the informal diners in the brasserie and the maximum of 60 lunches and 60 dinners the starred restaurant provides every day. Entering *La Rive* you are welcomed by the good-humored maître d'hôtel Maikel Ginsheumer, who heads his team in black in the typical Amstel way: correct, but with an informal verve where possible or required, ensuring that the culinary meeting between the guests and *La Rive* proceeds optimally. He also manages a Pandora's Box on wheels: the cheese trolley with delicacies from *affineur* Bernard Antony from Vieux-Ferrette, in the French Alsace, a specialist who will only supply the greatest chefs in Europe.

Sommelier Ted Bunnik operates in similar relaxed vein, with refined humor. His domain is an outstanding culinary component of *La Rive:* the atmospheric, dark and obviously climate controlled Wine Room (which can also be rented for a private dinner). The room houses wines of great distinction. It is a pleasure for Bunnik when a guest shows expertise by asking for an exceptional wine. "What do you think this wine

costs?" he asks in passing while selecting an expensive 1994 Grand Cru Romanée. I guess, incorrectly. "But do they at least finish it?" I ask with concern upon hearing the true price. "Certainly!" Ted assures me, knowing his guests, and without a sound he swishes 'up front' where the wine will be served with gracious portions of caviar.

Not just the style the hotel and restaurant staff exhibit on a daily basis, but also the location on the water must make the Amstel and *La Rive* so special to its guests – even if you are simply bobbing in the water in front of the door, on the banks of the river, for a conversation with the manager about the hotel business and culinary matters. Stepping back on shore, Beek extends a helping hand again. We enter *La Rive's* kitchen, passing the gleaming arsenal of cutlery and immaculately polished glassware. Second-in-command Dennis and photographer Bart laughingly raise their hands and from behind the pans Edwin approaches us enthusiastically. "Good, you're just in time, we were just starting with the sandwich of quail's eggs and vegetable quenelles!"

One of the most beautiful names for a truffle dish is 'chicken in partial – or full – mourning': flakes of black winter truffle are inserted under the skin of the animal, so that it looks as if the chicken is wearing a sober black coat. Dark slices of truffle also show through the potato spaghetti which Edwin Kats wraps around a fillet of turbot. It has become a signature dish, and with good reason. The chef: "Also very beautiful is the white truffle, which isn't really white but the color of sand or ochre, like an irregular potato. We serve it raw – to avoid spoiling its *profumo* – and always with earthy ingredients. Think of a creamy risotto, served with a fried free-range egg on top – the delicious truffle is shaved over it at the table."

Truffles

Of the hundreds of varieties of truffle found in nature, the black truffle *(Tuber melanosporum)* remains the best known, and is primarily found in Périgord and Umbria. Truffle hunting is usually done with trained pigs and dogs but swarming flies also mark many truffle locations, attracted by the good place to lay their eggs. Truffles are surrounded by an aura of luxury, created by their limited availability and erratic timing: a truffle decides for itself when it is ready to grow and when it is at its best. Like we humans, these recalcitrant subterranean fungi have good years and bad years, and sometimes they do not appear at all. Cultivating truffles is not an option: the mycelium (or hypha) does not allow itself to be forced into anything – it picks its own spot, often underneath an oak or hazel tree. It is possible, however, to apply the mycelium to the roots of a young tree, from which (God and the truffle willing) truffles can be harvested five years later.

Edwin Kats: "When we use black truffles it is always the fresh winter type, with its season stretching from November up to – and sometimes including – February: you can't define any exact limits, because the climate and local conditions have an enormous influence on the truffles. We don't use the black summer truffle, as we don't hold its taste in such high regard. We would rather use the winter truffle again, but then in a preserved form. You would need a trained palate to taste the difference. What is surprising is that truffle aficionados sometimes not only prefer the preserved truffles over summer truffles, but also prefer them over the fresh winter truffles. Still, in my opinion you can't beat the fresh variety." Several truffle dishes adorn the menu, and five of them found their way into this book. The black truffle finds itself in the company of (among others) rabbit with pearl onions ('marlouskes') and Limousin calf with fennel soufflé. The white truffle joins pig's cheeks, Savoy cabbage and creamed shallot. As we said: earthy ingredients.

Cassoulet of frogs' legs, white beans and beet with a hint of lime and black winter truffle shavings

For the sauce:
3.5 oz (100 g) bones from the frogs' legs
0.42 oz (12 g) shallot
0.88 oz (25 g) white wine
0.7 cups (1.75 dl) cream
0.8 cups (2 dl) poultry stock (see base recipes)
0.42 oz (12 g) lime juice
0.88 oz (25 g) truffle *jus*

9.8 oz (280 g) cleaned frogs' legs meat
28 shaped beet
4.2 oz (120 g) dried French white beans
or fresh white beans
1 tablespoon chopped chives
0.7 oz (20 g) black winter truffle
16 lime zests

Clean the frogs' legs and retain the bones for the sauce.

Sauté the bones and the shallot for the sauce in 0.35 oz (10 g) of oil, add the wine and allow to reduce. Add the cream, poultry stock and lime juice and allow the sauce to reduce to 0.8 cups (2 dl) over low heat. Strain the sauce and season with truffle *jus*.

Glaze the shaped beets.

Soak the white beans for 12 hours, and then slowly poach over low heat until cooked. The membrane on the beans should remain intact and become soft.

Heat a non-stick pan and sear the frogs' legs, then add the beans and half the sauce. Reduce the sauce until it binds. Add the beet and chives and arrange everything. Beat the remaining half of the sauce to froth with a hand blender and pour over the dish. Finish with the truffle (thinly sliced) and the lime zests.

Complex, aged white Graves and/or a rustic Pouilly Fuissé as a white wine
Moulin à Vent and/or Givry lightly chilled as a red wine

Braised cheeks and feet of free-range pigs with Savoy cabbage, creamed shallot, Jabugo ham and white truffle

INGREDIENTS FOR 4

4 free-range pig's cheeks
8 free-range pig's feet
4 cups (1 liter) veal stock (see base recipes)

For the pig's feet roll:
2.8 oz (80 g) meat from the pig's feet
1.4 oz (40 g) rind from the pig's feet
1.4 oz (40 g) goose liver *brunoise*
7 oz (20 g) reduced stewing liquid

5.25 oz (150 g) shallots
1.75 oz (50 g) half-whipped cream
2.1 oz (60 g) poultry stock (see base recipes)
4 Jabugo ham rosettes of 0.88 oz (25 g) each
5.6 oz (160 g) Savoy cabbage *bâtonettes*
4 dried Savoy cabbage leaves
0.7 oz (20 g) white truffle

Brown the cheeks and feet and cook in the veal stock for 3 hours over low heat. Allow the feet to cool and remove the bits of meat. Weight the required amount of meat, chop the rind, and keep the cheeks separately. Reduce 1.75 oz (50 g) stock to 0.7 oz (20 g), mix with the feet, rind and goose liver, and tightly wrap in cling film to form a neat roll. Allow the roll to stiffen in the refrigerator for 6 hours.

Clean the shallots, slice, and stew with the poultry stock. Blend to a smooth purée, heat this *à la minute* and mix with the half-beaten cream.

Blanch the 4 Savoy cabbage leaves, coat with olive oil and dry in an oven at 176°F (80°C) until crisp (leave the oven door ajar).

Stew the *bâtonettes* of Savoy cabbage with 0.35 oz (10 g) of butter.

Slice the roll into 4 equal parts and bread *à l'anglaise*, then sauté to a golden-yellow in 0.7 oz (20 g) peanut oil and 0.7 oz (20 g) butter.

Heat the cheeks in the stock. Arrange all the parts in a deep dish and finish with shaved white truffle and the dried Savoy cabbage leaves.

Solid, spicy rosé made from Grenache grapes
Supple, meaty Spanish red wine without 'Joven'-style wood aging

Roast rib of Limousin calf
with a soufflé of fennel and truffle,
and pink peppercorn and Parmesan sauce

INGREDIENTS FOR 4

To grease the moulds:
0.35 oz (10 g) soft butter
0.53 oz (15 g) grated Parmesan cheese

For the soufflé:
0.49 oz (14 g) butter
0.56 oz (16 g) flour
1.75 oz (50 g) cream
0.28 oz (8 g) truffle *jus*
1.05 oz (30 g) milk
1.4 oz (40 g) fennel puree
0.42 oz (12 g) chopped truffle
0.28 oz (8 g) fennel *jus*
0.21 oz (6 g) Parmesan cheese
1 egg yolk and 1 egg white

For the sauce:
0.35 oz (10 g) marrow
1.75 oz (50 g) shallot
1.23 oz (35 g) white wine
1 cup (2.5 dl) white veal stock (see base recipes)
0.5 cup (1.25 dl) cream
1.23 oz (35 g) grated Parmesan cheese
0.1 oz (3 g) pink peppercorn

2 eggplants
1.76 lb (800 g) calf's rib (if boned)
or 1.3 lb (600 g) (if boneless)

For the soufflés, carefully grease the moulds with soft butter and sprinkle with cheese.

Melt the butter and mix with the flour, cream, truffle *jus*, milk, fennel purée, truffle and fennel *jus*. Heat slightly. Remove the mixture from the heat and mix with the egg yolk. Beat the egg white with a pinch of salt and fold into the mixture. Next, fill the moulds just below the rim and bake *au bain-marie* for 45 minutes in a 284°F (140°C) oven. Remove the soufflés once they are properly puffed. After this, they can be warmed *à la minute* in an oven at 320°F (160°C), which takes approximately 6 minutes.

Halve the eggplants lengthwise, score and season with salt, pepper, a bay leaf, a sprig of thyme, a sprig of rosemary, a garlic clove and olive oil. Work the ingredients into the scores, wrap the eggplants in aluminum foil and cook for 40 minutes in an oven at 284°F (140°C). Allow the eggplants to cool, peel, and chop the meat, leaving to drain on a piece of kitchen towel. Heat *à la minute* and turn into *quenelles*.

For the sauce: melt the marrow over low heat, brown the shallots, add the wine and allow to reduce. Add the white veal stock, 0.07 oz (2 g) pink peppercorn and cream, and allow everything to reduce to 0.8 cups (2 dl). Strain the sauce and mix in the cheese with a hand blender. Do not heat the sauce again.

Remove the calf's rib from the refrigerator 2 hours before preparation. Heat a pan with 0.7 oz (20 g) of olive oil and sear the meat on both sides, adding 1.75 oz (50 g) of butter at the last moment and browning the meat in this one more time. Now cook the ribs for 20 minutes in an ovenproof dish, in an oven heated to 320°F (160°C). Allow the meat to rest in a warm place for 12 minutes, then remove from the bone and slice into pieces.

Arrange the *quenelles* and soufflé on top of the meat, with the sauce ladled around it, and garnish with a few shavings of pink peppercorn.

Wood-aged white Italian wine from Tuscany or a more southern wine region

Red Hermitage and/or spicy Syrah from the Languedoc

Warm ballotine of Dutch rabbit

with truffle, small shallots and green asparagus

INGREDIENTS FOR 4

2 whole saddles of rabbit, including liver and kidneys

For the stuffing:
2.8 oz (80 g) shoulder or leg meat
0.7 oz (20 g) egg
0.18 oz (5 g) bread crumbs
0.53 oz (15 g) rabbit liver *brunoise*
0.88 oz (25 g) minced truffle

For the sauce:
0.56 oz (16 g) shallot
2.4 cups (6 dl) white rabbit stock (see base recipes)
0.88 oz (25 g) white wine
0.42 oz (12 g) chopped truffle
0.53 oz (15 g) truffle *jus*

12 green asparagus
20 presentable small *marlouskes* (small shallots)
2.1 oz (60 g) poultry stock (see base recipes)

Ask the butcher for saddle of rabbit with a long flank. Debone the backs from the side, with the fillets remaining attached to the flank. Remove fillets from the least presentable back.

Mince the meat for the stuffing, and mix in a blender with the egg and bread crumbs until smooth. Lastly add the cream, and blend again. Remove the mixture and carefully blend in the truffle and liver.

Spread out the saddle with the 2 best-looking flanks and coat with the stuffing, lifting the 2 loose fillets into the other direction to ensure a well distributed, equal thickness. Now close the flanks and roll tightly in cling film. Tightly bind the roll with a piece of string, and poach for 45 minutes in water heated to 176ºF (80ºC). Remove the cling film and cut the roll into 12 neat slices.

Remove the membrane from the kidneys and lightly poach in 1.75 oz (50 g) rabbit stock for 5 minutes, at a heat of 158ºF (70ºC).

Peel the asparagus, blanch and stew *à la minute* with 0.35 oz (10 g) of butter.

For the sauce: brown the shallot in 0.18 oz (5 g) of olive oil, add the wine and allow the liquid to reduce. Add the stock and reduce to 0.6 oz (1.5 dl). Strain the sauce and use a hand blender to fix it with 20 g chilled pats of butter, truffle *jus* and walnut oil. At the last moment, carefully add the chopped truffle.

Clean the shallots and stew with 0.7 oz (20 g) butter and 2.1 oz (60 g) poultry stock.

Arrange the *ballotine* on a plate with the asparagus on top and the shallots next to it. Slice the kidney in two and arrange between the shallots. Pour the sauce between.

Young red Graves
Alsatian Pinot Noir, wood-aged
Buttery Meursault
Chardonnay from Chalônnais, perhaps not the first, certainly the best

Creamy truffle risotto with Parmesan cheese, a baked free-range egg and fresh, shaved white truffle

INGREDIENTS FOR 4

4 fresh free-range eggs

For the sauce:
1.4 oz (40 g) shallot
1 bay leaf
0.35 oz (10 g) dry sherry
0.35 oz (10 g) white wine
5.25 oz (150 g) poultry stock (see base recipes),
1.75 oz (50 g) veal stock (see base recipes)
5.25 oz (150 g) cream
0.7 oz (20 g) crème fraîche

1.05 oz (30 g) chopped shallot
3.5 oz (100 g) risotto rice
6.3 oz (180 g) poultry stock (see base recipes)
0.7 oz (20 g) truffle *jus*
2.1 oz (60 g) half-whipped cream
0.7 oz (20 g) grated Parmesan cheese
0.7 oz (20 g) fresh white truffle

Put away the 4 free-range eggs with the white truffle in a sealed container for 24 hours (the lovely truffle aroma will penetrate the porous eggshell).

For the sauce: lightly sweat shallots with the bay leaf in 0.18 oz (5 g) olive oil without browning, add the wine and sherry and allow to reduce. Add the poultry stock, veal stock, crème fraîche and cream and reduce to 0.8 cups (2 dl). Strain the sauce and beat to a froth *à la minute* with a hand blender.

Without browning, lightly sauté the shallot in 0.35 oz (10 g) peanut oil, add the risotto, pour over the poultry stock, and bring to a boil. Cover the pan with a piece of grease-proof paper and a lid. Place the pan in an oven preheated to 320°F (160°C), and cook for 16 minutes.

Season the risotto with salt, pepper, truffle *jus*, the half-whipped cream and the cheese. Arrange in a cutter of 4 inches (10 cm) in a deep dish.

Fry the free-range eggs in a non-stick pan, cut into circles (with a 4 inch or 10 cm cookie cutter) and arrange on top of the risotto. Finish the dish with a pinch of *fleur de sel* and shaved white truffle. Ladle the sauce around this.

Luscious, complex white wines from Tuscany or Piedmont
Aged Riesling from the Alsace

"For me, the asparagus border runs from Western Brabant to Roermond," proclaims Ad van Rooy, green grocer and supplier to *La Rive*. "South towards Limburg, the soil becomes too rich in lime, and that doesn't add to the taste of asparagus." For about a year Van Rooy has been delivering his top class produce to this restaurant on the Amstel; much to Executive Chef, Edwin Kats's, satisfaction, who, it goes without saying, only opts for the very best quality. "Ad gives me exactly what I want: perfectly formed AA extra, with a closed head, you won't find any better. We serve these asparagus within 24 hours of picking."

True connoisseurs ignore the all too premature greenhouse asparagus and wait until about the middle of May, when they appear from under the ground. Edwin Kats uses both white and green asparagus in his recipes. For the white, he trusts producers in the Brabant and Limburg provinces, but in early spring he has green asparagus brought in from the Perpignan area. These are Lorize asparagus, named for their subtle taste and exterior 'feminine line', produced by farmer Robert Blanc. These reach their best taste if the temperature remains at 21ºC for seven days. This way, the typically lush, sweet flavor can be experienced to the full.

Asparagus

Kats: "I love that seasonal character – I really try and retain that. Every year I enjoy the asparagus season anew; not only because of the fantastic taste, but also because asparagus are much healthier than most people think."
Low in calories and free from cholesterol, asparagus contain various minerals such as calcium, phosphorus and iron, and, on top of that, offers a large store of vitamins (B, C, E and K). Potassium and saponins ensure that asparagus have a beneficial effect on our water retention and kidneys. The taste of the Queen of the Fields, the amino acid, asparagine, also helps with its diuretic functions (and causes the lingering asparagus 'odor'). Knowing all this, you might want to live by the traditional Dutch adage that you need 'per mond een pond'... a pound per mouth to feed.

Asparagus *(Asparagus officinalis)* have been appreciated as the ultimate late spring treat since Greek and Roman times. In his encyclopedic works, naturalist Pliny the Elder wrote of wild asparagus growing in 'northern Germania in the mountains and fields'. Wild asparagus can also be found in the Netherlands: in the Kennemer dunes near Haarlem you can immediately spot the fine, feathered leaves; in autumn the plants sport bright red berries. Asparagus have a short season: true to tradition, harvesting stops on 24 July, St. John's feast day. That gives plants the opportunity to regain their vigor... just in time for the next spring.

Crispy roasted asparagus
with a salad of spring vegetables,
vinaigrette of Vin Santo vinegar and truffle

INGREDIENTS FOR 4

Peel the asparagus and boil until cooked in ample salted water, allow it to cool in the liquid and dry thoroughly between two cloths.

Bread the asparagus anglaise and fry in peanut oil until crisp, adding 1.75 oz (50 g) fresh butter near the end. Allow the asparagus to drain on paper towels, and season with a little salt.

String the green peas and broad beans, blanch the peas and beans and remove the skins. Also blanch the French beans or *haricots aiguillettes*, celeriac and spring turnip. Peel the bunched carrots with a thin peeler, then slice into neat strips and blanch as well.

Create an attractive salad by mixing all the vegetables, the various types of salad and the herbs, dress with some vinaigrette, salt and pepper and arrange on a cutter with the asparagus.

Optional: add some chopped truffle.

For the vegetable salade:
20 asparagus stalks (AA extra)
5.25 oz (150 g) green peas
12.25 oz (350 g) broad beans
2.6 oz (75 g) *haricots aiguillettes* or French beans
3.5 oz (100 g) bunched carrots
3.5 oz (100 g) *mange-tout* (pod peas)
12 celeriac bulbs
12 spring turnip bulbs
Variety of salad types (*mizuha, cordifole, frisée* or curly endive and dandelion)
fresh green herbs
(chervil, chive tips and tarragon)

For the vinaigrette:
1 tablespoon balsamic vinegar
1 tablespoon Vin Santo vinegar
2 tablespoons asparagus bouillon
2 tablespoons walnut oil
1 tablespoon truffle *jus*
1 tablespoon regular olive oil
1 tablespoon extra virgin olive oil

 Vernaccia di San Gimignano, light white wine, somewhat oxidative with soft, smoky fruit

Lukewarm asparagus spaghetti with grilled, lightly smoked East Scheldt lobster, garlic fritters and lemon thyme

INGREDIENTS FOR 4

2 East Scheldt lobsters of approximately 500 g
8 thick asparagus stalks (AA)
0.6 cups (1.5 dl) lobster *coulis* (see base recipes)
4 slices of Parmesan cheese
12 cloves of garlic
1 lemon
3 sprigs lemon thyme
ᴗᴗ
peanut oil to deep-fry

Bring *court-bouillon* to the boil (see base recipes), add the lobster, bring to the boil again, remove pan from the heat and allow the lobsters to cool in the pan. Remove the lobster meat from the shell (the *coulis* can be prepared using the heads).

Heat a smoking pan with 0.35 oz (10 g) of wood chips, and when the pan is smoking properly place the grill with the lobster on it and allow it to smoke for 2 minutes.

Remove lobster from the grill, brush with 0.35 oz (10 g) of olive oil, and lightly grill over charcoal.

Peel the asparagus, halve, cut into thin slices, and subsequently slice these into thin strips. Heat oil in a pan and slowly fry the asparagus spaghetti with 0.53 oz (15 g) of butter. Do not allow the asparagus to lose their color!

Bring the *coulis* to a boil and allow the sprigs of lemon thyme to steep for 3 minutes. Using a hand blender, fix the *coulis à la minute* with 0.7 oz (20 g) chilled butter.

Place the slices of Parmesan cheese in a preheated oven of 320°F (160°C) and roast until crispy for 6 minutes.

Clean the garlic cloves and cook slowly in 0.4 cups (1 dl) milk until done.

Coat the cloves with fritter batter (see base recipes) and deep-fry at 347°F (175°C) until golden yellow.

Place the spaghetti at the center of a plate. Arrange the lobster on top, surrounded by the *coulis* and 3 fritters. Garnish with the Parmesan cheese *tuiles* and a thin slice of lemon.

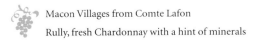

Macon Villages from Comte Lafon
Rully, fresh Chardonnay with a hint of minerals

Asparagus tips in cream with poached free-range egg, morels and broad beans

INGREDIENTS FOR 4

24 asparagus stalks (AA extra)
4 very fresh free-range eggs
0.8 cups (2 dl) organic vinegar
26.25 oz (750 g) broad beans
1 sprig savory
7 oz (200 g) fresh morels
2 cups (5 dl) cream

Peel the asparagus and cut the tips at 2.8 inches (7 cm), then halve lengthwise.
Bring 8 cups (2 liters) of water with 0.8 cups (2 dl) of organic vinegar and 2.1 oz (60 g) salt to a boil. Break the fresh eggs into a cup, use a whisk to form an eddy or vortex in the nearly boiling water, and carefully transfer the eggs into this. Allow the eggs to cook slowly for about 2 minutes. Rinse the eggs in a pan with warm water, handle with care and put aside.

Shell and blanch the broad beans, then remove the skins.

Remove the stems from the morels, halve lengthwise, and wash them carefully in lukewarm water. Leave them to dry on a cloth.

Boil the asparagus tips in cream, and season with salt. Remove them from the cream when done.

Heat 0.35 oz (10 g) olive oil in a pan and steam the morels with 0.7 oz (20 g) of fresh butter until done, then add the broad beans and some chopped savory. Season the vegetables with salt and pepper.

Arrange the asparagus on top of each other on a deep plate, place the poached egg on top, and surround with the morels and broad beans. Pour a teaspoon of the cream used to prepare the asparagus over the egg.

Smaragd wines from Austria
Buttery, rustic, ripe Meursault

'Pot au feu' of glazed veal shank with asparagus and spring vegetables

INGREDIENTS FOR 4

1 veal shank
16 cups (4 l) white veal stock (see base recipes)
20 asparagus tips of 2 inches (5 cm)
3.5 oz (100 g) mange-tout (pod peas)
5.25 oz (150 g) green peas
12.25 oz (350 g) broad beans
2.6 oz (75 g) *haricots aiguillettes* or French beans
3.5 oz (100 g) bunched carrots
12 spring onions
8 slices of glazed artichoke

freshly picked green herbs like purslane, chervil, chive tips, tarragon, coriander, sage and parsley

Ask the butcher to cut the shank on both sides, so that can stand upright.

Poach the shank in white veal stock over a low heat for approximately 3 hours.

Remove the shank from the poaching liquid and stand it upright in a fire-proof dish. Place the dish in a preheated oven at 320°F (160°C) and baste the shank with a ladle of poaching liquid every 5 minutes. Repeat until the liquid has formed a nice glaze (takes about 45 minutes).

Clarify the remaining veal stock and save to serve with the dish.

Shell the green peas and broad beans, blanch and remove the skins. Also blanch the beans, spring onion and snow peas. Peel the bunched carrots with a thin peeler, then cut into neat strips and blanch.

Pick the herbs and store in the refrigerator.

Remove the shank from the bone and cut into thin slices, heat the asparagus and present like a cutter. Heat the vegetables and finally mix with the green herbs. Arrange the vegetables in the center of the asparagus, surrounded by the shank and pour the clear veal bouillon over the shank.

Pinot noir from the Thermen region of Austria,
red wines full of fruit and slightly mineral with a hint of sweetness

Edwin Kats

Edwin Keats

Make no mistake about people from Brabant. Behind their candid joviality and broad smiles a burning ambition often hides. So, do not be fooled by Edwin Kats. Of course he is warm, likeable and relaxed, as you would expect of someone from Brabant. However, on the shop floor he is the boss, or, as it has been called in gastronomy for centuries now, the chef. On the floor and in the 'aquarium' – his little glass office at the center of the large kitchen – he reigns, concentrated, with a natural authority. His robust appearance and sometimes compelling green eyes do help: a meaningful look or brief comment here, a quip with an ironic undertone there. In this domain of flickering knives, searing hot stoves and whirling cooks, he sets the tone through his effort, knowledge and ambition; also by expecting as much energy and dedication from his chefs as he gives. When the first orders start coming in around half past seven and Edwin starts announcing them, "chef!" and "oui!" can be heard from his team. Raising his voice? That is never necessary.

Every chef starts by learning to cook. For the 12 year-old Edwin Kats from Oosterhout this started at a youth camp. The camp leader had to prepare a daily meal for 25 people. Edwin assisted, noticed how much he liked it, and without a moment's hesitation changed his field of study the moment he arrived back home.

At breakneck speed, he followed every conceivable course in the hotel and catering field, received diplomas ranging from Presentation Technique to Kitchen Management, from Apprentice to Master Chef. On 1 July 1985 Edwin Kats started his career as third- and fourth-year student in the *Kurhaus* in Scheveningen. Later he worked as fifth-year student at *Le Bouc* in the town of his birth, and rose to the rank of *sous chef.* Next he became *chef de partie* at the Hotel Restaurant *Corona* in The Hague, and in 1992, under Robert Kranenborg, he was taken on as junior *sous chef* in the elite corps of *La Rive,* with its two Michelin stars. Edwin: 'Kranenborg had also been the chef at Corona, and with him and five others I went along to La Rive.' Kats stayed there for two years, gathered an overwhelming amount of experience, and took that along to *de Swaen* in Oisterwijk (1 Michelin star), where he became *chef de cuisine* under Cas Spijkers. An ambitious leap to *Vermeer* (in the Barbizon Palace Hotel in Amsterdam)

Make no mistake about people from Brabant. Behind their candid joviality and broad smiles a burning ambition often hides. So, do not be fooled by Edwin Kats. Of course he is warm, likeable and relaxed, as you would expect of someone from Brabant. However, on the shop floor he is the boss, or, as it has been called in gastronomy for centuries now, the chef. On the floor and in the 'aquarium,' – his little glass office at the center of the large kitchen – he reigns, concentrated, with a natural authority. His robust appearance and sometimes compelling green eyes do help: a meaningful look or brief comment here, a quip with an ironic undertone there. In this domain of flickering knives, searing hot stoves and whirling cooks, he sets the tone through his effort, knowledge and ambition; also by expecting as much energy and dedication from his chefs as he gives. When the first orders start coming in around half past seven and Edwin starts announcing them, "chef!" and "oui!" can be heard from his team. Raising his voice? That is never necessary.

Every chef starts by learning to cook. For the 12-year-old Edwin Kats from Oosterhout this started at a youth camp. The camp leader had to prepare a daily meal for 25 people. Edwin assisted, noticed how much he liked it, and without a moment's hesitation changed his field of study the moment he arrived back home.

At breakneck speed, he followed every conceivable course in the hotel and catering field, received diplomas ranging from Presentation Technique to Kitchen Management, from Apprentice to Master Chef. On 1 July 1985 Edwin Kats started his career as third- and fourth-year student in the Kurhaus in Scheveningen. Later he worked as fifth-year student at Le Bon in the town of his birth, and rose to the rank of sous chef. Next he became chef de partie at the Hotel Restaurant Corona in The Hague, and in 1992, under Robert Kranenborg, he was taken on as junior sous chef in the elite corps of La Rive, with its two Michelin stars. Edwin: 'Kranenborg had also been the chef at Corona, and with him and five others I went along to La Rive.' Kats stayed there for two years, gathered an overwhelming amount of experience, and took that along to de Swaen in Oisterwijk (1 Michelin star), where he became chef de cuisine under Cas Spijkers. An ambitious leap to Vermeer (in the Barbizon Palace Hotel in Amsterdam)

followed; with his *sous chef* Dennis Kuipers he attained a Michelin star. From 16 July 2000 he has been back on base as Executive Chef at *La Rive*, still rightfully sporting two glorious stars.

In any conversation with Edwin Kats he emphatically brings his 'sous' to the foreground. He would prefer even more to refer to 'his chef' when the conversation turns to Dennis Kuipers (32) from Delft, descendant of a family of barge skippers. Kuipers was his second-in-charge at *Vermeer*, and came along to *La Rive*. Edwin: 'Without Dennis the world would have been a very different place. Over the years we've come to anticipate each other's actions. Our characters are quite different, but that almost seems like a prerequisite to forming a good team. Dennis is exceptionally dedicated and driven. When I'm really beat, he will say: "Shall we continue for just a while longer?" He also has much more patience with the guys than I do; he makes a very good coach. Perhaps I'm more the creative mind of the two, but Dennis is perfect at executing ideas.'

On the shop floor the difference between the two does not seem that big – they are a smoothly running machine and half a word or gesture appears sufficient – but the difference can be seen in their respective attitudes. Whereas Kats appears dead calm, Dennis is a mass of whirling energy. While Kats is the man of the moment, of the here and now, Dennis dreams of opening a small countryside hotel with his wife (who is a pastry chef) 'one day'. Their sources of inspiration differ too. When it comes to favorite cookbooks, Kats prefers the works of Alain Ducasse and Dennis immediately opts for *White Heat* by Marco Pierre White. What they do share, forming the solid basis for their collaboration, is mutual respect; sometimes unspoken, at other times expressed heartily. And their burning ambition speaks for itself. Dennis: "From the very start it was clear to me that I could strive for a second star with Edwin. And when we indeed achieved the second one, we simply looked at each other and knew without saying it: very well, we'll continue together and see where the limit is."

Edwin Kats is not a man for swaggering bravura or big words, but when he enters the imposing lobby of the Amstel Hotel to meet you, you see a personality filling the space. 'I want to create something in my field', he says in conversation, seemingly without emphasis. It is a straightforward sentence from such a young chef (at 34). Once you get to know him better, you know this statement to be his guide in life, his motivation to be present around nine every morning and, basically, being the last to turn off the lights at night.

He would not often show himself in the 'front' of the restaurant. ("Who am I to parade there and accept the honor while there are 35 of us working?") But he does want to know who to expect that evening. Not only to shake the hand of a distinguished guest, but possibly to offer something special – quietly, without fanfare from his kingdom at the back. As chef of *La Rive,* but also as the person who has final responsibility for everything concerning banqueting (from room service breakfasts for hotel guests to catering in the historic saloon boats of the Amstel) he just wants to be informed. Nobody need fear an extravagant gesture, that's not in his nature. But he wants to know. Even if there are no VIP guests present, one always has the impression that an examination is taking place in Kats' kitchen. Kats: "We owe it to our guests to strive for a ten every day. Actually, I'm not satisfied with less than a nine."

The Executive Chef hails from Northern Brabant, where his mother worked in the health sector and his father was a carpenter. The style of cooking for the Kats family (Edwin, his parents and younger sister Wendy) was very much Dutch, just as in the case of Dennis. Now and then his mother would try new dishes; as in so many families introduced by mother but seldom embraced by father. Kats, grinning: "When my parents ate here at *La Rive,* my father said: 'Delicious, son, but your mother does the potatoes much better, nice and crumbly.' I can accept that, you know. My mother cooks with a lot of love and attention; practically never any junk food, and also no frozen goods or canned vegetables. Fresh was her motto." A chef could have worse schooling.

These values are reflected in his cooking and he demonstrates – armed with his knowledge, love and experience – his preference for simplicity, for dishes sublime in their effortlessness. Having 'marlouskes' (cocktail onion) on his menu is a subtle reference to his Brabant roots. It is true that his croquettes of salted cod now come with oysters and a *quenelle* of caviar, but on his level that is hardly any surprise. Yet, level or not: it matches. Add another typical Kats expression: "The tastes should go together. There should be a reason for combining ingredients. Not simply throwing something together, but asking yourself why you're doing it. I learned that from Robert Kranenborg. He's the kind of chef that wakes you up. Because of his enormous knowledge of food, he knows everything about flavor combinations. He stimulates you to think, to pay attention to detail, and not to assume everything but to explore the philosophy behind a dish. Fortunately, I met him when I was about 22, which is the age at which you are open to the subtleties of taste. I made quite a lot of notes then, and many of my own recipes are still based on that."

On 26 January 1588, under the picture of a new plant, the botanist Charles l'Ecluse (also known as Carolus Clusius) wrote: "Small truffles (*taratoufli*), received from Philippe de Sivry in Vienna." A charming mistake or an accurate observation? The great botanist was not the only person to compare this tuber from the New World with truffles; its name reflects another relationship: *taratoufli* became *Tartoffel*, which became the German *Kartoffel*. Yet many people initially remained unconvinced about the spud's nutritional value, let alone being bowled over by the taste, related to the truffle or not. Only a few individuals spoke up in favor of the potato, like the famous German 'spud preachers', ministers who used their pulpits to advise congregations to plant the tuber with its blue flowers and dark green leaves. So it went for centuries; when grain crops failed, people relied on potatoes, more for its nutritional value than for taste. For how long was it fashionable to denigrate the potato, food of the people? Especially in restaurants? Apart from enthusiasts and experts, it took until the end of the 20th century before the potato conquered (or re-conquered) restaurant menus in all its glory, and managed to win over chefs. Today, early into the 21st century, a menu without at least one dish containing La Ratte, Roseval, Purple Congo, Opperdoezer Ronde, Belle de Fontenay or Truffle potato(!) would be unthinkable. At last, after 415 years, Carolus Clusius's 'mistake' has a new power of expression. In short: the potato has come full circle.

Potatoes

The German-Russian tsarina Catherine the Great was a big supporter of the potato. She realized that the simple tuber, which soon yielded large crops, could feed millions of hungry mouths. As a culinary honor, a potato dish was named after her: *Pomme de Terre Czarina* (sometimes called *Pomme de Terre Catharina*), naturally served with sour cream and a dab of caviar. (For caviar purists, potatoes – or blini, slightly risen buckwheat pancakes – are the only way to consume the delicacy.) The combination of exquisite roe with the humble spud is so sublime, that the greatest chefs will always opt for this prelude. And so Edwin Kats offers potato flapjacks with smoked salmon, cucumber and caviar. He logically chooses Osetra caviar with its nutty taste – perfect with real buckwheat blini or the warm taste of potatoes (like Nicola).

A remarkable dish from Kats's kitchen (often mentioned in culinary guides) is turbot wrapped in potato spaghetti (prepared from Platat nr. 4, ideal for French fries) from which slices of truffle shine through. His La Ratte mousse is also notable: this variety of potato has an irregular elongated shape (affording it the nickname 'asparagus potato'), and appears to have a built-in hint of brine. A presentation of such a mousse with a tartar of wild oysters and green asparagus completes the circle – of potato history and current events, but also of good taste and the art of combinations.

Cannelloni of potato and smoked salmon with cucumber and Osetra caviar

INGREDIENTS FOR 4

For the potato pancakes:
8.8 oz (250 g) pureed potato
1 cup (2.5 dl) milk
0.7 oz (20 g) melted butter
1 egg
0.2 oz (6 g) salt
2.1 oz (60 g) flour

12.6 oz (360 g) smoked salmon
1 cucumber
3.5 oz (100 g) crème fraîche
0.1 oz (2 g) chopped chives

For the cucumber jelly:
1 cucumber
1 pinch of chlorophyll (see base recipes)
3 gelatin leaves (or 3 teaspoons of gelatin powder)

32 sprigs of dandelion
1 oz (28 g) caviar (Osetra)
20 sprigs of chervil
20 drops of dressing

Mix the potato puree with the milk, butter, egg, salt and (lastly) the flour. Stir well until a smooth mass is formed. Heat some peanut oil in a non-stick pan and fry the pancakes.

Allow the pancakes to cool, and cut into squares of 4.7 by 4.7 inches (12 by 12 cm). Spread these with crème fraîche, sprinkle with chives and then add the smoked salmon. Carefully turn over and roll tightly. Now roll the cannelloni in plastic, and allow it to stiffen in the refrigerator for 4 hours.

Peel the cucumber for the jelly, slice into pieces and blend with the chlorophyll. Allow the moisture to drain on a cloth, then bring the moisture to a boil and dissolve the soaked gelatin. Pour the mixture into a shallow bowl and leave to set in the refrigerator for 6 hours. Remove the resulting jelly from the dish and cut into neat blocks or in rounds.

Flute the remaining cucumber (see base recipes), slice in half lengthwise, chase and blanch. Pick the dandelion leaves and wash well.

Trim the cannelloni straight on both ends and fix a strip of cucumber to each side; around that, arrange the blocks of jelly, dandelion sprigs, drops of dressing and chervil, and divide the caviar equally among the cannelloni.

Sauvignon Blanc from New Zealand or the Neusiedlersee in Austria
Mumm de Cramant Champagne

La Ratte potato mousse with tartar of oysters and herbs, potato tuile, slices of smoked salmon and green asparagus

INGREDIENTS FOR 4

For the *tuiles:* mix the potato puree with all other ingredients and allow it to thicken in the refrigerator. Roll out the dough on greaseproof paper and bake for 6 minutes at 356°C (180°C). Remove the *tuiles* from the oven, use a small cutter to cut some circles, and shape these on a ring.

For the mousse: peel the potatoes and boil with salt in 4 cups (1 l) of water. As soon as the potatoes are done, retain 0.4 cups (1 dl) of liquid and discard the rest. Blend the potatoes and retained liquid in a blender until smooth. Now add the dissolved gelatin and leave it to set on icy water. Whip the cream and mix in the mascarpone. As soon as the potato mass starts to set, add the cream and fill the cutters with the mousse. Place the cutters in the refrigerator and allow it to set for at least 6 hours.

Open the oysters, preserving the liquid, and mix with the fish fumet; clarify the liquid and mix with the dissolved gelatin (a ratio of 0.8 cups or 2 dl liquid to 0.2 oz or 6 g gelatin). Slice the oysters carefully, mix with the *fines herbes* and the jelly, and spread the tartar over the potato mousse; be sure that the mousse has set properly.

Peel the green asparagus, blanch, cut the tips at 2.8 inches (7 cm) and halve. At the center of the platter place the *tuile* surrounded by the mousse, around that the slices of smoked salmon, combined with the asparagus in-between and a few drops of herb oil.

For the potato tuile:
5.25 oz (150 g) potato puree
1 egg
0.2 cups (0.5 dl) milk
0.88 oz (25 g) melted butter
0.88 oz (25 g) flour

For the potato mousse:
6.5 oz (185 g) peeled La Ratte potatoes
0.4 cups (1 dl) cooking liquid
1½ leaves of gelatin
(or 1½ teaspoons of gelatin powder)
4.4 oz (125 g) cream
0.2 oz (6 g) salt
0.5 oz (15 g) mascarpone

12 wild Brittany oysters
1 tbs *fines herbes* (see base recipes)
0.8 cups (2 dl) fish fumet (see base recipes)
12 green asparagus stalks
10.5 oz (300 g) smoked salmon
2 tsp herb oil (see base recipes)

South African Chardonnay from a cool district, Franschhoek, for example
Chablis Premier Cru or Grand Cru

Croquettes of salted cod, potato and Bélon oysters, creamy sauce of young leeks and Osetra caviar

INGREDIENTS FOR 4

For the salpicon:
5.25 oz (150 g) dry potato puree
1 egg yolk
2.6 oz (75 g) *brunoise* potato
4.7 oz (135 g) cooked salted cod
12 Bélon oysters (size 1)
~

For the sauce:
2.5 oz (70 g) white of leek
0.25 oz (7 g) shallot
0.35 oz (10 g) Noilly Prat
0.2 oz (6 g) white wine vinegar
0.5 oz (15 g) white wine
0.4 cups (1 dl) fish fumet (see base recipes)
2.5 oz (70 g) cream
~

1 leek to dry
1 oz (28 g) Osetra caviar
~

peanut oil to deep-fry

Wash the potatoes well, place in the oven on coarse sea salt and bake for 75 minutes at 320°F (160°C). Allow the potatoes to cool slightly and then halve, remove puree from the peel and force through a strainer while still warm. Blanch the *brunoise* potato, allow it to drain on a cloth and mix with the potato puree, cod and yolk.

Season to taste with freshly ground pepper.

Allow the *salpicon* to cool and divide into portions of 1.23 oz (35 g). Open the oysters and dry on a cloth. Flatten the *salpicon* in the palm of your hand and add 1½ oyster, fold the *salpicon* over and roll into a neat, firm croquette.

Finely chop the leek and shallot for the sauce, brown in 0.35 oz (10 g) oil and deglaze with the white wine vinegar, Noilly Prat and white wine. Allow the liquids to reduce and add the fish fumet and cream. Simmer the sauce for 6 minutes, blend and strain.

Clean the leek and blanch the leaves, rub with olive oil and cut in strips of 7.9 inches (20 cm) long and 0.3 inches (8 mm) wide. Dry these in an oven of 176°F (80°C) until crisp.

Bread the croquettes *à l'anglaise* and deep-fry in peanut oil, allow it to drain and put on a strip of potato puree. Arrange a *quenelle* of 0.25 oz (7 g) of caviar between the croquettes. Complete the dish with the warm sauce and 3 ribbons of dried leek.

Sauvignon blanc from Marlborough, New Zealand
Mild, ripe Riesling
Albariño from Galicia (Spain)
Young Chablis
Crémant Champagne

Creamy potato soup and nutmeg
with goose liver ravioli and celery

Sauté the leek and blanched celery for the soup, add the potatoes, the bouquet, the stock and the cream.

Allow everything to cook well, remove the bouquet and blend the soup, then strain.

Blanch the potato *brunoise*, pour over the 12 small slices of goose liver, add a celery leaf on top and cover with the large slices of goose liver.

Heat the ravioli in an oven at 248ºF (120ºC) for 2 minutes.

Blanch the potato slices and arrange on a deep plate, add the ravioli and some celery *chiffonade* in-between.

Ladle the soup over the garnish and sprinkle a small amount of nutmeg.

INGREDIENTS FOR 4

For the potato soup:

8.8 oz (250 g) peeled Nicola potatoes
2.8 oz (80 g) chopped blanched celery
1.75 oz (50 g) chopped leek
8.8 oz (250 g) poultry stock (see base recipes)
12.25 oz (350 g) cream
1 bouquet of 2 slices smoked ham, 1 bay leaf,
1 sprig thyme, 1 sprig rosemary

4.2 oz (120 g) potato *brunoise*
12 potato slices
12 celery leaves for the ravioli
12 celery leaves for the *chiffonade*
12 slices goose liver of 1.2 inches (3 cm) thick
12 slices goose liver 2.4 inches (6 cm) in diameter
Nutmeg to taste

Turbot and truffle wrapped in potato spaghetti with stewed Swiss chard and light veal gravy

INGREDIENTS FOR 4

2.2 pounds (1 kg) potatoes, suitable for French fries
4 x 5 oz (140 g) turbot fillets cut from turbot (n° 1)
1 oz (28 g) fresh black truffle
21 oz (600 g) Swiss chard stems
1 tomato, peeled
20 sprigs of picked chervil

For the sauce:
0.3 cups (0.75) dl fish fumet
0.3 cups (0.75) dl poultry stock (see base recipes)
0.2 cups (0.5) dl veal stock (see base recipes)
0.7 oz (20 g) pats of chilled butter
0.35 oz (10 g) extra virgin olive oil

Shape the potatoes into balls and roll them through a pasta machine into long spaghetti. Rinse the spaghetti in cold water and blanch briefly, without breaking them! Season the turbot fillet with salt and pepper and cover with truffle (0.25 oz or 7 g per portion). Tightly wind the potato spaghetti around the turbot fillet.

Cut the beet green stems into batonettes, blanch in fast-boiling water and stew *à la minute* with a cube of butter.

Reduce the fish fumet, poultry stock and veal stock together to 0.4 cups (1 dl), and fix with olive oil and chilled butter.

Heat oil in a non-stick pan until very hot, place the turbot in the pan and fry on both sides until crispy (approximately 3 minutes per side). Add 1 oz (30 g) of butter during the last 20 seconds.

Slice the peeled tomato into *chinoise* and arrange on a platter; between the *chinoise* place sprigs of chervil. Dress the beet greens in the center of the platter with the turbot on top. Surround with the sauce, beaten to froth.

Bellet from Provence
Condrieu, from a year that was not too light
White Graves, ripe to well aged

Perhaps because he was a fisherman himself for ten years, nobody needs to tell Aart Schouten – from Eurofish in Den Oever – where to buy his fish. Schouten has excellent relations with the 'small fishermen', who go out on a cutter with a small crew. And that makes for short lines, to stick to fishing terms: caught today and on the plate at *La Rive* tomorrow is not an exception for Eurofish but rather the standard practice. Many of the fish on offer at *La Rive* are caught locally. Schouten: "Most of the time our fishermen are located nearby, for example in the 'Texelse Stenen'. Cod are sometimes caught so close to shore you could throw a ball onto the beach." The season is an important determining factor: when certain types of fish migrate, Schouten travels along as far as possible; for example 'to the south', to the auction in Breskens, to get hold of the last bass. Edwin Kats: "The fish we order by phone in the evening are ready in the kitchen the following morning. For foreign types of fish and a backlog, for example of turbot and pike perch, we can always count on Schmidt Zeevis. It occasionally happens that we are unexpectedly caught without – ordering is an art form as well – but even for a kilogram of turbot or tongue they will make a special delivery."

Crustaceans and shellfish

Although King crab, North Sea crab and scallops are very much allowed on Kats's stage, he regularly accompanies fish dishes with vegetables and greens (such as asparagus and Swiss chard), or indeed shellfish: fillets of sole, for instance, are served with subtle lobster-filled tortellini. Kats: "I would say langoustines are my favorite crustacean, and with shellfish, my favorite would be scallops, supplied to our kitchen by Plaisir de la Table, a supplier that makes quality a priority. The *coquilles St. Jacques* come from Dieppe, and the langoustines from Loctudy. Oysters are supplied by expert Ron Reitsma, at home in Brittany since the age of 15. We use mussels as well, of course: for soups and sauces we use the regular *Zeeuwse* from Zeeland, and, when in season, we serve mussels harvested from *bouchot* poles, from the bay of Mont St. Michel."

Supplier Reitsma: "The oysters for *La Rive* come from parks ranging from Carnac to the Charante, like the flat Bélon, named after the river Bélon where it is cultivated. The small oysters are known for their taste: smooth and creamy rich. The *fine claire* can be called a straightforward oyster – what you see is what you get." Not surprising then that Kats royally incorporates them in an equally straightforward, but refined, dish: grilled *coquilles St. Jacques* with cauliflower gratinée, potato sauce and tartar of *fines clairs* in *fines herbes...*

Dry, baked coquilles St. Jacques with a fresh goat's cheese and basil mousse, and sweet-and-sour pumpkin and onion compote

INGREDIENTS FOR 4

Soak the gelatin for the goat's cheese mousse in water; dissolve the goat's cheese in the warm milk, and add the gelatin. Leave on iced water until the mass becomes lumpy, and then add half-whipped cream and chlorophyll. Mix carefully so that the mousse becomes marbled by the chlorophyll.

Lightly sauté the pumpkin in 0.35 oz (10 g) oil, add curry powder, and finally add tomato and onion. Cover with a lid and stew the mixture over low heat until cooked, then remove from the heat and add the maple syrup, honey and vinegar. Cook to evaporate the remaining vapor and store chilled.

Wash the salads and herbs well, pick and leave to dry on a cloth. Dress with 0.35 oz (10 g) extra virgin olive oil just before serving. Brown the scallops in 0.53 oz (15 g) of hot olive oil, then bake for 4 minutes in an oven at 338°F (170°C).

Squirt a line of mousse on the plate with a pastry bag, arrange *a quenelle* of pumpkin compote on either side, decorate with salad at the center, and finally position 1 scallop. Finish the dish with the drops of dressing and pumpkin seed oil.

For the goat's cheese mousse:
3.5 oz (100 g) fresh goat's cheese
2.1 oz (60 g) milk
2.1 oz (60 g) cream
1 egg yolk
2 gelatin leaves (approximately 2 teaspoons)
basil chlorophyll (see base recipes)

For the sweet-and-sour pumpkin:
8.8 oz (250 g) pumpkin brunoise
4.4 oz (125 g) onion
3.5 oz (100 g) tomato
0.04 oz (1 g) curry powder
1.4 oz (40 g) maple syrup
0.35 oz (10 g) honey
0.53 oz (15 g) champagne vinegar

Attractive, small herb salad of dandelion, *frisée* (curly endive), mizuha, chervil, shiso purple, chives and tarragon
16 equal-sized sea scallops, at 0.88 oz (25 g) each
A few drops of dressing (see base recipes) and pumpkin seed oil

Dry white Loire made from Chenin Blanc grapes
Lugana

Salad of North Sea crab prepared with green herbs, served with lemon gingersnaps and a spicy gazpacho

Blanch the finely cut lemon. Mix all ingredients for the lemon *tuiles* and leave the batter to stand in the refrigerator overnight. Smoothly blend all ingredients in a blender and allow it to drain on a cloth until it reaches the right consistency. Moisture should not be draining from the mixture any more.

Roll out a thin layer of the *tuile* dough and bake on a sheet of greaseproof paper for 6 minutes at 338ºF (170ºC). Cut the *tuiles* with a cookie cutter and leave these to harden on a cold surface.

Lightly fry the crêpes without coloring them, and cut into circles smaller than the *tuiles*.

Mix the crab meat with the mayonnaise and the *fines herbes*, and divide into 12 equal portions. Distribute these among the crêpes and stack with the *tuiles* (the crêpes serve to prevent the *tuiles* from going soft).

Mix all ingredients for the gazpacho together, pour the gazpacho into the plates and smoothen with the curved side of a spoon. Use a pastry bag to place 8 dots of crème fraîche on the rim of each plate.

For the lemon tuiles (lemon gingersnaps):
0.53 oz (15 g) fine *brunoise* of lemon rind
2.6 oz (75 g) white castor sugar
1.23 oz (35 g) all purpose flour
1.05 oz (30 g) butter
0.53 oz (15 g) water

For the gazpacho:
7 oz (200 g) tomato flesh
3.5 oz (100 g) peeled canned tomatoes
2.1 oz (60 g) reduced crab *coulis*
(see base recipes)
0.88 oz (25 g) onion
1.23 oz (35 g) peeled, red sweet pepper
1.05 oz (30 g) cucumber flesh
0.07 oz (2 g) garlic
0.14 oz (4 g) allspice
0.1 oz (3 g) ginger
0.28 oz (8 g) sherry vinegar
0.42 oz (12 g) sesame oil
0.42 oz (12 g) grape seed oil
0.18 oz (5 g) *hoisin* sauce
0.28 oz (8 g) soy sauce
0.07 oz (2 g) lime juice
1 drop Tabasco

9.8 oz (280 g) crab meat
12 small egg crêpes: 2 eggs and 0.7 oz (20 g) cream
2.8 oz (80 g) mayonnaise (see base recipes)
0.14 oz (4 g) *fines herbes* (see base recipes)
1.75 oz (50 g) whipped crème fraîche,
mixed with a pinch of chlorophyll
(see base recipes)

Sémillon wine from Margareth River, Australia

Sauvignon from a wine district with a sultry climate, for example, a Bernardus from Monterey and/or St. Valentin from Alto Adige

Grilled coquilles St. Jacques with cauliflower au gratin, tartar of oysters and green herbs, and potato sauce

INGREDIENTS FOR 4

12 sea scallops

4.2 oz (120 g) small cauliflower florets

To gratinée the cauliflower:

5 egg yolks

3.5 oz (100 g) gastric (see base recipes)

2 tablespoons extra virgin olive oil

1.75 oz (50 g) whipped cream

3.5 oz (100 g) potato puree

12 wild oysters

0.14 oz (4 g) *fines herbes* (see base recipes)

For the sauce:

3.5 oz (100 g) Nicola potatoes

0.42 oz (12 g) shallot

0.88 oz (25 g) white of leek

8.8 oz (250 g) fish fumet (see base recipes)

1.75 oz (50 g) cream

1 tablespoon red wine vinegar

Cut the cauliflower into small florets and blanch.

Open the oysters, chop and leave to dry on a cloth. Mix *à la minute* with the *fines herbes*.

Slice the potatoes, shallot and leek for the sauce, sauté in 0.35 oz (10 g) olive oil, add the wine vinegar, fumet and cream, and boil the potatoes until cooked. Blend the sauce and strain.

Rub the scallops with oil and grill on a hot grill plate, then bake 4 minutes in an oven at 320°F (160°C).

Beat the eggs and the gastric *au bain-marie* until well bound, fix with the olive oil and allow it to cool. Finally mix with the lightly whipped cream.

Heat the cauliflower florets and place in a cutter (1.2 inches or 3 cm), cover with a spoon of *gratinée* liquid and *gratinée* the florets in a hot oven.

Squirt the potato puree in a cutter (1.2 inches or 3 cm) and fill with the oyster tartar.

Arrange the 3 scallops on a plate with a cauliflower tartlet and a potato-oyster tartlet in-between. Pour the sauce around this.

White wine, not wood-aged, from the Côtes de Provence, Cassis

White Château-Neuf-du-Pape, as young as possible

Poached fillet of sole with lobster tortellini, corn and grilled sweet pepper tartlet, and beurre blanc with lime and thyme

INGREDIENTS FOR 4

Mix the flour with the salt, then with the olive oil and egg yolks. Knead the dough well and make sure it becomes smooth, which can of course also be done with a mixer.

Cut the corn from the cobs; combine with the milk and strain. Dilute the corn milk with flour, eggs, butter and salt to become a batter.

Bake the crêpes and cut 16 circles of 1.2 inches (3 cm) in diameter. Peel the sweet peppers and remove the seeds and stems. Sauté the sweet peppers in the peanut oil over low heat (about 176°F or 80°C). When they look attractive after 1 hour, remove them and grill on one side. Also cut the sweet peppers into circles of 1.2 inches (3 cm).

Roll the pasta dough into a thin sheet and cut circles of 4 inches (10 cm), placing a piece of lobster (0.25 oz or 7 g) on each circle. Spread the rim of each circle with egg yolk and fold over, bringing both ends together and pinching. Slowly poach the tortellini à la minute in 1 liter of water with 0.7 oz (20 g) salt and 0.7 oz (20 g) olive oil until cooked.

Rub the fillets of sole with olive oil, and salt lightly. Also coat 4 pieces of aluminum foil with olive oil. Place the fillets on the oily aluminum and roll tightly, carefully twisting both ends to close tightly (as with a piece of candy).

Bake the fish rolls for 8 minutes in an oven at 320°F (160°C). Make the corn and sweet pepper tartlets, each consisting of 2 layers of corn, 2 slices yellow and 2 slices red sweet pepper, arranged round and round.

Mix the gastric with the cream and slowly add the chilled pats of butter. Add 3 drops of lime juice and a sprig of thyme at the last moment. Strain and dish up the *beurre blanc.*

Place the rolled fillet of sole at the center of the plate, with the tortellini and vegetable tartlets around it. Place 4 lime zests and 1 sprig of thyme on each fillet. Place a piece of popcorn on top of each of the vegetable tartlets.

For the pasta dough:
1.75 oz (50 g) hard pasta flour
1.75 oz (50 g) all purpose flour
3 egg yolks
0.07 oz (2 g) fine sea salt
0.18 oz (5 g) olive oil

For the crêpes:
4 cobs corn
2 cups (0.5 liter) milk
4.7 oz (135 g) flour
2.1 oz (60 g) melted butter
3 eggs
0.42 oz (12 g) salt

For the beurre blanc:
6 tablespoons gastric (see base recipes)
1.5 teaspoons cream
3.5 oz (100 g) chilled pats of butter
3 drops lime juice
1 sprig thyme

1.2 lb (550 g) fillet of sole
4.2 oz (120 g) lobster meat
(from 1 lobster of about 1.1 lb, or 500 g)
16 circles of candied red sweet pepper
16 circles of candied yellow sweet pepper
2 cups (0.5 liter) peanut oil,
to sauté the sweet pepper
8 kernels popped, salted popcorn
16 lime zests
4 sprigs thyme

White St. Aubin
Chablis Premier Cru
Chardonnay from the Penedès
White Mas de Daumas

Slices of smoked salmon
with a salad of lobster, North Sea crab,
shrimp and fine vegetables

INGREDIENTS FOR 4

7 oz (200 g) smoked salmon flank (Bawykov)

2.1 oz (60 g) Dutch shrimps

2.1 oz (60 g) North Sea crab meat

2.1 oz (60 g) lobster meat

(from a lobster of about 8.8 oz or 250 g)

For the vegetable salad:

8 strips bunched carrot

4 slices baked, green zucchini

4 slices artichoke

4 slices cooked fennel

4 dried leek ribbons

12 *cordifole* leaves

12 *mizuha* leaves

poultry stock (see base recipes)

For the vinaigrette:

0.35 oz (10 g) lime juice

0.35 oz (10 g) white wine vinegar

1.05 oz (30 g) extra virgin olive oil

1.05 oz (30 g) grape seed oil

0.7 oz (20 g) reduced lobster *coulis*

(see base recipes)

Boil the whole fennel bulb in lightly salted water. Once cooked, cut the fennel into thin slices. Cut the zucchini into thin lengthwise slices; first grill on a hot plate, and then cook for 2 minutes in an oven at 302°F (150°C). Peel the artichokes and cut the bottoms into thin slices. Glaze the 'closed' slices (those without holes) with poultry stock. Peel the bunched carrots with a thin peeler, then cut into attractive strips and blanch. Pick the leek and blanch the leaves, coat with olive oil and cut into strips of 4 inches (10 cm) long and 0.3 inches (8 mm) wide. Dry the strips in an oven at 176°F (80°C) until crisp. Cut the back of the salmon into neat slices of 0.2 inches (0.5 cm) thick.

Construct the tartlet of vegetables, crab, lobster and shrimp on the plate in this order: a slice of artichoke, zucchini, shrimp, fennel, *mizuha*, crab, bunched carrot, *cordifole*, lobster and then leek. Arrange the salmon next to the tartlet like a roof tile, and evenly pour around the vinaigrette.

Chenin Blanc, Loire from a ripe harvest, but vinified dry

Mild New Zealand Riesling

South African white from Franschhoek (a cool region)

'Sautéed Miéral duck with all its trimmings' is what Edwin Kats calls one of his poultry dishes. This explains the chef's all-embracing love for producer Miéral ("I was really impressed when I first received and tasted their poultry"). Kats not only uses the duck's more traditional breast and drumsticks, but also the stomach, heart and liver, and even the sweetbreads – fried a lovely golden yellow. Such a duck passes me from the very busy restaurant kitchen on its way 'out front', smelling of exquisitely roasted meat and presented in a soberly effective way. If there is one dish that demonstrates what Kats wants for his kitchen, this must be it. "We have a classic focus, with contemporary elements and a no-frill presentation", says the chef. 'Classic' can only mean French. And as Kats prepares it, with all its trimmings, outside of *La Rive* a Miéral duck like this can probably only be found in France.

Poultry

La qualité, rien que la qualité: quality, nothing but quality. Since 1919 this has been the motto of French poultry producer Miéral from Montrevel, in the Bresse district between the Sâone and Ain rivers. (This is a region where – slightly nationalist – the French *tricolore* can be recognized in the poultry: the red comb, the white feathers and the blue legs.) For four generations, Miéral has been dedicated to producing top quality animals, having initially started out by producing 'regular' butter, eggs and chickens. This is Kats's supplier for guinea fowl and ducks, the *Canettes de Barbarie Excellence Miéral:* free-range animals that feed on herb-filled pasture, with supplementary feed similar to that of the famous Bresse poultry. Around the age of 13 or 14 weeks the ducks start molting. Only four or five weeks after the change of plumage does Miéral find the taste of the animals up to standard. A week of hanging adds even more *goût* to the meat, and only then is it sold to clients such as *La Rive*.

The pigeons used in Kats's kitchen are also French (Anjou Royal), but the Netherlands and Belgium also produce excellent poultry. Flanders offers the chef its famous *Mechelse koekoek*, a free-range chicken before the fact: as early as 1801 a chicken with feathers like a cuckoo is mentioned; in 1895 the breed was protected and certified by the Belgian *koekoeksclub* (the National Organization for Agrarian and Horticultural Heritage). White, juicy and marbled meat (permeated with tiny fatty deposits) is characteristic of the *Mechelse koekoek.* Nearly identical to this chicken (but without the so-called 'socks', its feathered feet) is the Dutch Blue, surprisingly enough supplied by Paul and Carla de Wit in Sint Laureins in Belgium, and one of the best types of chicken currently available – understandably, as the Dutch Blue is given the time to grow fat in peace and quiet. And that shows in the taste.

Poached 'Anjou Royal' pigeon, corn crêpes filled with goose liver and creamy black pepper sauce

INGREDIENTS FOR 4

4 Anjou pigeons
4.2 oz (120 g) goose liver
20 spring onions

For the crêpes:
4 cobs of corn
2 cups (0.5 liter) milk
4.7 oz (135 g) flour
2.1 oz (60 g) melted butter
3 eggs
0.42 oz (12 g) salt

For the sauce:
3.5 oz (100 g) pigeon carcasses
0.53 oz (15 g) shallot
0.1 oz (3 g) bruised black pepper
0.12 cups (0.3 dl) white wine
0.8 cups (2 dl) pigeon bouillon
0.8 cups (2 dl) cream

4 cups (1 liter) pigeon bouillon to poach the pigeon
0.35 oz (10 g) of butter

Clean the pigeons and sauté the drumsticks in goose fat over low heat.

Once the drumsticks are done, scrape them clean and sauté until crispy.

Slowly poach the breast in the bouillon at 162ºF (72ºC).

Cut away the corn from the cob; blend with the milk and strain. Dilute the sauce with the flour, butter, eggs, and salt.

Bake the pancakes in a non-stick pan and cover with slices of goose liver, sprinkle with salt and pepper and cut them into circles (using a small bowl or a large cookie cutter).

For the sauce, let the pigeon carcasses with the shallot and pepper sweat in a pan, deglaze with the wine, add the bouillon and cream, and allow everything to simmer until the sauce thickens.

Strain the sauce when done.

Clean the spring onion and blanch, then stew *à la minute* with 0.35 oz (10 g) of butter.

Remove the meat from the pigeon carcass and slice neatly. Place a crêpe on the plate, arrange the pigeon on this, place the crispy drumsticks on the pigeon breast and arrange the spring onions at the center. Spoon the sauce around the food.

 Wines made from the Merlot grape, such as Saint-Emilion

Sautéed Miéral duck with all trimmings, sweet-and-sour spring turnip and purslane

INGREDIENTS FOR 4

1 Miéral duck
1.1 lb (500 g) goose fat to sauté
3 extra duck stomachs and 3 extra duck hearts
20 spring turnip bulbs
〜

Glazing liquid consisting of 1 oz (30 g)
honey vinegar
2.6 oz (75 g) poultry stock (see base recipes)
1.75 oz (50 g) honey
〜

24 sprigs of summer purslane
〜

For the vinaigrette:
4 tablespoons reduced duck stock
(see base recipes)
1 tablespoon almond oil
4 tablespoons extra virgin olive oil
2 tablespoons honey vinegar
Milk

Detach the drumsticks from the duck and sauté in goose fat for 3 hours at 176°F (80°C). Remove the bones from the drumsticks and allow the meat to slowly fry to a crisp on its fatty side.

Clean the hearts and stomachs and rinse in cold water for 1 hour, then fry in goose fat for 2½ hours at 176°F (80°C). Remove the sweetbreads from the neck and rinse well. Remove the liver and soak in milk for 24 hours.

Now proceed to clean the duck, leaving the breast on the carcass. Use the remaining pieces to make the duck stock.

Remove the duck from the refrigerator 2 hours before using, and let it stand to reach room temperature. Heat some goose fat in a pan. Rub the goose breast with salt and pepper, place the duck in the pan breast down, and sauté over low heat until the skin turns crisp. Subsequently, place the duck in an oven of 338°F (170°C) for 6 minutes, and then keep warm.

Stew the spring turnips in the duck stock until done.

Heat the stomachs and hearts in some goose fat; heat the drumsticks and sauté the liver and sweetbreads in some oil until golden brown. Remove the duck's meat from the carcass and carve into strips.

Arrange the garnish on top of the spring onion bulbs, and in front of this place the strips of duck breast and the purslane dressed with vinaigrette.

Ladle an additional spoon of vinaigrette over the dish.

Dolcetto d'Alba
Chinon
Domaine de Marotte Vieilles Vignes from the Ventoux

Roasted Miéral guinea fowl with baked salsify, Vin Santo sauce and nutmeg

INGREDIENTS FOR 4

2 bound Miéral guinea fowl
4 long salsify (oyster plant), to boil
1 long salsify (oyster plant), to sauté
Peanut oil, for sautéing

For the sauce:
2.1 oz (60 g) guinea fowl wings
0.88 oz (25 g) shallot
0.7 oz (20 g) white wine
0.42 oz (12 g) Vin Santo vinegar
0.6 cups (1.5 dl) veal stock (see base recipes)
1 cup (2.5 dl) poultry stock (see base recipes)
0.7 oz (20 g) chilled butter pats
ground nutmeg to taste

0.7 oz (20 g) butter

Peel the salsify and boil in milk. Leave to cool, and subsequently cut into pieces of 2 inches or 5 cm (6 pieces per person).

Wash the one salsify well and cut into thin strips with the skin on. Deep-fry the strips in peanut oil at 320°F (160°C) until golden yellow and crisp, then salt lightly.

Remove the guinea fowl from the refrigerator and leave for 3 hours to reach room temperature. Rub the fowl with salt and pepper, and sauté each drumstick in 0.35 oz (10 g) olive oil for 15 minutes over low heat. Now sauté the fowl until golden brown all over, bake in an oven of 356°F (180°C) for 15 minutes and store in a warm place.

Chop the wings for the sauce into small bits, add the shallots and allow everything to brown slowly. Add the wine and Vin Santo vinegar and allow to evaporate; add the veal and poultry stock, and reduce the liquid to 0.6 cups (1.5 dl). Strain the sauce, fix with 0.7 oz (20 g) chilled butter and season to taste with ground nutmeg.

Sauté the salsify to a golden yellow in the 0.7 oz (20 g) butter and arrange on the plate. Cut the meat from the guinea fowl carcass and arrange next to the salsify. Place the deep-fried salsify on top and finish the dish with the sauce.

Full-bodied Côte de Nuits
Barbaresco or Rosso di Montalcino

Roasted Dutch 'Blauwpoot' chicken with Jabugo ham, sautéed chicory and a creamy oloroso sherry sauce

INGREDIENTS FOR 4

4 Dutch 'blauwpoot' chickens, with skin
2 neat slices of Jabugo ham
2.8 oz (80 g) thinly slices Jabugo ham
4 slices pork crépine (caul fat)
10 heads chicory
3.5 oz (100 g) butter and 0.35 oz (10 g) sugar

For the sauce:
2.8 oz (80 g) minced chicken wings
0.53 oz (15 g) finely sliced shallot
1.4 oz (40 g) oloroso sherry
2 dl poultry stock (see base recipes)
0.6 cups (1.5 dl) cream
0.7 oz (20 g) goose fat

0.4 cups (1 dl) oloroso sherry

Rinse and soak the pork *crépine* for 24 hours.

Loosen the skin on one side of the fillet, season with salt and pepper and cover with the sliced ham. Replace the skin and wrap the fillet with the *crépine*.

Roast the 2 slices of ham between 2 layers of greaseproof paper in the oven at 248ºF (120ºC) until crisp, approximately 25 minutes. After the slices come out, cut them into 4 thin strips.

Clean the heads of chicory and stew until done with 0.7 oz (20 g) butter and some water. Once done, remove the heads from the pan and halve lengthwise. Sauté in a non-stick pan and fry with the butter and sugar until a nice golden brown, caramelizing the sugar in the process.

Carefully brown the breast fillets in 0.7 oz (20 g) goose fat, and then roast in an oven of 266ºF (130ºC) for a further 12 minutes. Carve the fillets *à la minute*. For the sauce, brown the wings and shallot slightly, deglaze with the sherry, and allow the sherry to reduce, add poultry stock and cream and allow everything to reduce by half. Strain the sauce and beat *à la minute* with a hand blender until frothy.

Reduce 0.4 cups (1 dl) of sherry until the liquid becomes syrupy.

Place the sliced breast portions next to each other, beside the heads of chicory, with the sauce and a few drops of sherry in-between. Finish the dish with the crispy Jabugo ham.

Rioja, lightly wood-aged and full-fruited
Pinot Noir, Mercurey or Fixin for example
Possibly wood-aged white from the Graves

Moments
of pleasure

Moments
of pleasure

For many of the citizens of Amsterdam, as well as for guests from outside the capital, the Amstel and *La Rive* are an ideal resting place, to be cherished and returned to time and again. When actress Ellen Vogel was asked where in Amsterdam she could best relax, she unequivocally replied that the Amstel was her favorite spot for unwinding in polished refinement. Of course, Ellen Vogel is not the only famous person in the Netherlands to take pleasure in the *La Rive* restaurant or its stylish wine room for intimate dining, surrounded by hundreds of top wines from around the world. "Every guest must experience a visit to *La Rive* as the purest pleasure, that's what we aim for" – this is the motto of the black and white-clad restaurant team.

Every now and then the chef and his team like to come up with a special attraction. Guests, for example, can reserve a seat at the chef's table. At the center of the kitchen the cooks present an eight-course menu with specialties prepared in front of the invited guests, the best way to sample the atmosphere backstage at a decorated restaurant and its kitchen.

The wine room also serves as the backdrop to a number of theme evenings, which are often influenced by seasonal products. An aperitif with asparagus treats on the salon boats of the Amstel starts off an evening filled with culinary delights, where courses are interspersed with talks on the background and uses of the vegetables.

As a top hotel and restaurant, it follows naturally that the already spoilt guests are given just that little bit extra. Such a highlight is the catering on the historic salon boats: during a trip on the Amstel guests are served a complete dinner, prepared à la minute, while enjoying Amsterdam's beautiful network of canals. Upon their return, guests often finish off this unique excursion in the hotel lounge over an exquisite bottle of wine or an aromatic cigar from the humidor.

For many of the citizens of Amsterdam, as well as for guests from outside the capital, the Amstel and La Rive are an ideal resting place, to be cherished and returned to time and again. When actress Ellen Vogel was asked where in Amsterdam she could best relax, she unequivocally replied that the Amstel was her favorite spot for unwinding in polished refinement. Of course, Ellen Vogel is not the only famous person in the Netherlands to take pleasure in the La Rive restaurant or its stylish wine room for intimate dining, surrounded by hundreds of top wines from around the world. "Every guest must experience a visit to La Rive as the purest pleasure, that's what we aim for," – this is the motto of the black and white-clad restaurant team.

Every now and then the chef and his team like to come up with a special attraction. Guests, for example, can reserve a seat at the chef's table. At the center of the kitchen the cooks present an eight-course menu with specialties prepared in front of the invited guests, the best way to sample the atmosphere backstage at a decorated restaurant and its kitchen.

The wine room also serves as the backdrop to a number of theme evenings, which are often influenced by seasonal products. An aperitif with asparagus treats on the salon boats of the Amstel starts off an evening filled with culinary delights, where courses are interspersed with talks on the background and uses of the vegetables.

As a top hotel and restaurant, it follows naturally that the already spoilt guests are given just that little bit extra. Such a highlight is the catering on the historic salon boats: during a trip on the Amstel guests are served a complete dinner, prepared à la minute, while enjoying Amsterdam's beautiful network of canals. Upon their return, guests often finish off this unique excursion in the hotel lounge over an exquisite bottle of wine or an aromatic cigar from the humidor.

Ted Bunnik, sommelier

It was the music festival known as the *Nijmeegse Vierdaagse* that dragged Ted Bunnik, the son of a lumber dealer, into the hospitality industry. Very reluctant, I agreed to work as a waiter in a friend's outdoor café. I immediately liked the work, not only because of the informal atmosphere but also for the ease with which I was able to do it.'

This event made the well-spoken, polite son of Nijmegen (born there in 1957) give up his first love: acting. He had attended the acting schools of Arnhem, Maastricht and Antwerp, but left the stage without regret. Through the official route of on-the-job training as waiter in a restaurant he joined the team in black, and worked at *Val Monte* in Berg en Dal. His acceptance as a fifth-year student to the renowned and (then) quite classic *Excelsior/de l'Europe* was far from traditional and showed courage: "I simply went in, asked the maître d' for work, and got it." In 1980 Bunnik came to the Amstel: "To be honest, I thought it was a hospital – let alone knowing they had their own excellent restaurant! A real timid boy from the provinces! The head waiter predicted a difficult application process ('you'll probably have to fillet a chicken or eel') but I was appointed without any problem."

Bunnik: "At *La Rive* I rose by another rank and became *chef de rang*, at which you are allowed to wait on some tables by yourself. Those were very different times. I remember that the chef back then, Becu from Zeeland, used to throw torpedoes, you know, those big silver serving trays." With a straight face: "What he didn't count on was that I would simply throw them back." The Amstel Hotel had to make do without a wine master for some years. Ted: "Everyone pitched in, but in 1992 the new management at *La Rive*, chef Kranenborf and host Vincke, asked me to specialize in that field. And I'm still doing it, with an exceptional amount of pleasure." Bunnik says it with modesty, as if it is odd that they would want him in particular, but his skill, verve and way with guests are respected by everyone. It is clear why he has reached one of the highest positions attainable in the hospitality industry, that of sommelier. And it is typical that he mentions his master teachers here, Hubrecht Duijker and Robert Kranenborg.

Each bottle of wine served has been judged, ordered and tasted by Bunnik. Also the 1994 Echezeaux Grand Cru (Domaine Romanée Conti, at € 395,00), which some guests nonchalantly order to accompany a portion of caviar. Ted, sensibly: "An excellent choice." Only one out of every 12 wines he tastes, Bunnik selects for the excellent Wine Room, his wine domain, where you may dine as a small group, as with the Chef's Table in the kitchen. 'Apart from the house wine and house champagne, with which more colleagues are involved, I decide on the wines on offer. Together with members of the team and the chefs, we decide on how best to use such a wine. That's a never-ending search. I find it a challenge to dare to shift borders when it comes to selecting wine. I also regularly ask the guests: "What do you think of it?" I'm in the enviable position of doing what I really enjoy and working with great professionals."

"The nice thing about Edwin Kats is that, when he's composing his menu, he keeps in mind the wines I select or recommend using in sauces, which, after all, are a chef's signature. It sometimes takes up to a year before you find a good combination. On top of that, from his classic French foundation Kats has been experimenting more and more, meaning that we can do really beautiful things regarding taste experiences and harmonious combinations of wine and food."

The sommelier's favorite wines

White wines:
Château Pape Clement 1979;
this wine was the breaking point
Grüner Veltliner Smaragd 1997, Hirtzberger, Wachau;
resistance is useless
Bellet 1999 Château de Cremat;
not easy, but extremely worthy of the cuisine
Veuve Clicquot Champagne; for personal reasons
Sauvignon Blanc Isabel Estate, Marlborough, New Zeeland; and you thought you knew this grape

Red wines:
Château Haut Brion 1ᵉʳ Grand Cru Classé Graves;
any time, any place
Vega Sicilia Unico, cuvee without vintage, Ribera del Duero; blending raised to an art form
Sforzato Alberada Valtellina; strange guys, these Italians, winning hearts and livers
Collioure le Seris Domaine de la Rectorie;
how France obtained a New World Wine
Château Trotanoy Pomerol;
for taking to a desert island, instead of a book

Cigars at La Rive

As is the case with products used in the kitchen or wine, quality is an important factor when choosing cigars. The standards of quality are already set by the producers, who only use the best quality tobacco leaves during production. In consultation with our suppliers, a choice worthy of *La Rive* is made from their selection. Clearly the Cohiba collections may not be left out: more specifically, the best cigar in the world, namely the *Cohiba Esplendidos*. Also present are *Davidoff Anniversario, Montecristo A* and *Partagas*, with their 8-9-8 (25 pieces in three layers) and their Series D n° 4. Three series of the world famous Dutch brand *Hajenius* can also be found in our humidor. The *Sumatra* series, renowned for its aromatic smoothness, with as highlight the cigar of the millennium, the *Corona Naturel Special;* the *Grand Final* series with an extra dose of Havana and Brazil for the somewhat fuller body; and the *HBPR* series, a fully handmade long filler made in the old Nicaraguan tradition, can be provided.

The degree of humidity in which cigars are kept (between 70 and 75% normally, and around 55% for Dutch-made cigars) is very important to guarantee their quality. At *La Rive* the cigars are checked for quality on a daily basis. The *La Rive* humidor consists of four layers, and the humidity can be measured and set separately for each layer.

A good cigar needs time. Between production and presentation to the consumer at least six months should pass. Many guests see smoking a cigar as a ritual to conclude an enjoyable dinner. At *La Rive* a neutral flame is usually used, like cedar wood or a gas lighter: matches and candles give off a taste or some wax, to the detriment of the cigar. By rotating the end over the flame and simultaneously drawing air through the cigar, the smoke canal is warmed uniformly, preventing it from burning. The cigar is only lit when the whole fired end is burning. The Amstel Hotel provides the guest with the opportunity to enjoy the taste of his cigar.

"I don't want them any bigger than this." Edwin Kats rolls his hands into a ball, his fingertips touching each other. He is indicating the size of the goose livers he requires, never overly proportioned, always from animals that – at least compared to the regular goose, or the average chicken – have led a respectable life. The selection he entrusts to Milan Schutte of Fine Food Milan, a supplier with a reputation to uphold with these livers – they actually come from free-range geese bred by small, independent farmers.

Domestic geese *(Anser anser)* were kept by the ancient Egyptians for their meat and liver. The Romans also kept these vigilant animals, as described by Pliny. There is a famous tale of how an alert gaggle of geese warned the Romans of a surprise attack on their capitol in 4 AD.

Goose breeding now takes place in many parts of the world, like Hungary, where they can boast of an age-old tradition. As soon as the geese develop their plumage, they are sent outside to find their own food, protected against the cold or harsh sun by the shade of shrubs and trees. During the *gavage*, the feeding period, they regularly eat a limited amount of cooked corn (a maximum of 0.68 fluid ounces or 20 cc) for three weeks. Such a leisurely pace eventually results in a liver of around 1.1 pounds (500 grams), about 3.5 ounces (100 grams) more than in nature (but two to three times smaller than in the case of intensive farming methods). Due to its smaller size, the Hungarian goose liver is proportionally more expensive, but the welfare of the animals is worth every cent. And so say the farmer, the supplier and the chef.

Goose liver

A restaurant with the status of *La Rive* is obliged to serve goose liver, but Kats would not want it any other way, taken as he is with variety meats. A long time ago – and how strange is it to speak of 'long ago' with such a young chef – he composed a dish of goose liver: *terrine de jambon 'Jabugo' et foie d'oie en gelée de queue de boeuf au poivre de Séchuan* – a wonderfully constructed terrine in subtle layers. A standard ingredient is a product the chef loves working with: Jabugo ham from the Spanish Huelva, and then preferably the leg of this beautiful, quite slim, grayish-black pig (*pata negra ibérico*, literally the Iberian black leg) which loves eating bellotas, the acorns of the cork oak. This is tender dried ham, with a strong spicy taste and fresh overtones.

Kats combines the Jabugo with thin slices of blade steak and goose liver, in an oxtail jelly with Szechuan pepper (the exquisite type from China, a country where geese feature in innumerable fables). The different structures of the types of meat are fully recognizable, and the tender membranous nature of the liver completes the dish. The terrine is very much Edwin's signature, which he took with him from *de Swaen* and to *Vermeer*, the restaurant in Amsterdam that he – with his second chef Dennis - won a star for. Now it can also be found on the menu at *La Rive*, printed in gold, the hallmark of his signature dishes.

Terrine of Jabugo ham, goose liver and stew steak with oxtail jelly and Szechuan pepper

INGREDIENTS FOR **10**

10.5 oz (300 g) thinly sliced goose liver
1.3 lb (600 g) thinly sliced and fried stew steak
1.1 lb (500 g) Jabugo ham
1.6 cups (4 dl) oxtail jelly
0.21 oz (6 g) bruised Szechuan pepper
30 sprigs of shiso purple
30 tarragon tips
30 sprigs of chervil

Stew a whole piece of stew steak until done and cut into thin slices.

Cut the goose liver into thin slices in the same way.

Also slice the Jubago ham in this way.

Ensure that the fat from the ham and tendon from the stew steak have been removed.

Line a terrine mould with plastic, and start constructing the terrine.

Spread some oxtail jelly between slices, and continue until the terrine mould has been filled. This should take approximately 3 hours (for a trained maker). Leave the terrine to set overnight, and cut into neat slices of 2.8 oz (80 g) each. Allow the remaining jelly to set, and chop. Fill a pastry bag with the chopped jelly and squirt into a narrow circle on a chilled plate. Garnish the jelly rim with the sprigs of herbs. Position the slice of terrine at the center.

Pinot Gris, Jurançon Doux as white wine
Ribera del Duero and Collioure as red wine, not too old, not too woody and slightly chilled

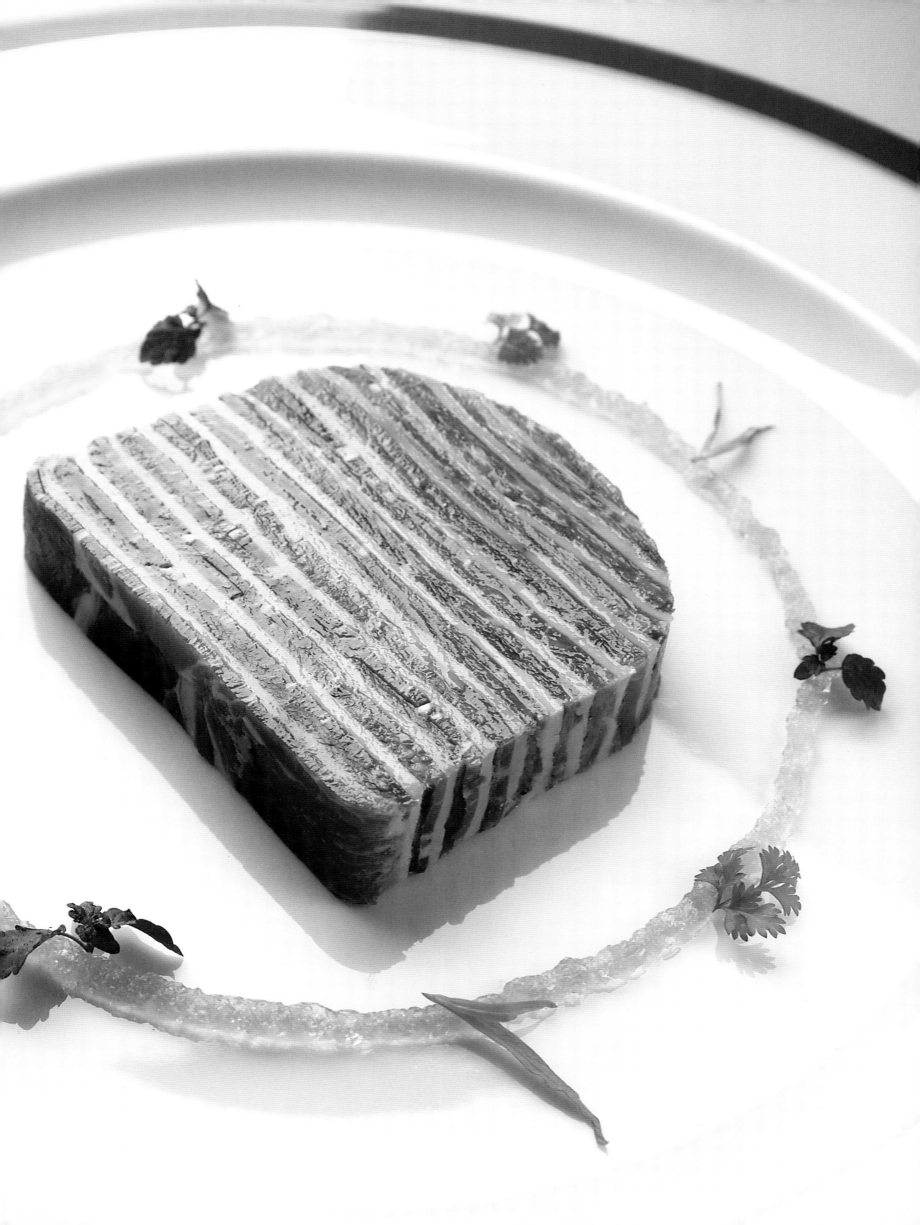

Goose liver gratinée with duxelles of mushrooms, cubes of calf's tongue and escargots, with aged Madeira sauce

Slice all the mushrooms to the same size *brunoise* and fry lightly without browning, leave to cool and mix with ham, *fines herbes*, bread crumbs, cream and soft butter.

Brown the goose and liver and allow to cool, season with salt and pepper, and cover with a thin layer of the gratin.

Blanch the zucchini pearls and stew *à la minute* with the spring onion, calf's tongue and the snails in 0.53 oz (15 g) fresh butter.

Sauté the cuttings and shallots for the sauce without browning in 0.35 oz (10 g) peanut oil, deglaze with Madeira, add the veal stock and reduce slowly. Fix the sauce with 0.53 oz (15 g) chilled pats of butter.

Place the goose liver slices in an oven heated to 392°F (200°C) and bake for 4 minutes. Arrange the goose liver in the center of a plate, surrounded with the garnish. Dress the sauce on the plate.

INGREDIENTS FOR 4

8 slices of goose liver
1.4 oz (40 g) per slice

For the duxelles:
5.25 oz (150 g) *brunoise* of various mushrooms (shiitake, porcini, wood hedgehog, oyster mushrooms, *agaricus augustus* or the 'Prince')
1.75 oz (50 g) finely sliced ham
0.07 oz (2 g) *fines herbes* (see base recipes)
0.39 oz (11 g) fresh bread crumbs
0.7 oz (20 g) soft butter
0.35 oz (10 g) cream

20 poached snails

For the sauce:
1.05 oz (30 g) beef trimmings
0.7 oz (20 g) chopped shallot
1.4 cups (3.5 dl) veal stock (see base recipes)
2.6 oz (75 g) aged Madeira

48 green zucchini pearls
48 spring onion *chinoise*
2.8 oz (80 g) calf's tongue *brunoise*

Wines from the Libournais district: Fronsac, Néac or Madiran (10 year-old Bouscassé)

Salad of pig's feet, goose liver and truffle, with a dressing of petits pois and celery

Brown the pig's feet and cook in the veal stock over low heat for 3 hours. Allow the feet to cool slightly and remove the bits of meat.

Heat the goose fat to 176°F (80°C), immerse the goose liver and leave to stand for 20 hours. Take the liver out, remove excess fat, and cut into 20 neat slices.

Blanch the julienned vegetables and dress with the salad and 0.7 oz (20 g) vinaigrette. Arrange the salad in a cutter.

Sprinkle the bits of pork with bread crumbs, and heat in a hot oven for 1 minute or gratinée under a hot salamander.

Arrange a piece of pork on each slice of goose liver, surround with the vinaigrette and the peas, celery leaves and the drops of dressing.

INGREDIENTS FOR 4

4 pig's feet
3.2 cups (8 dl) veal stock (see base recipes)
0.35 g (10 g) fresh bread crumbs
7 oz (200 g) goose liver
1.1 lb (500 g) goose fat to sauté the liver
2.8 oz (80 g) vinaigrette (see base recipes)
1.75 oz (50 g) julienned carrot
1.75 oz (50 g) julienned celeriac
1.75 oz (50 g) picked *frisée* (curly endive)
2.1 oz (60 g) double-shelled green peas
Chiffonade of 10 celery leaves
40 drops of dressing (see base recipes)

Riesling from the Alsace region, 'Grand Cru'-style as a white wine

Pinot noir, wood-aged and from the Alsace, or light Côte de Beaune Crozes Hermitage as red wine

Goose liver baked in a fig and nut brioche with a red port and clove sauce

Mix all ingredients for the brioche (except the butter) and knead in a food processor. Add the butter in small pats at the very last. Keep kneading the dough for another 10 minutes, and add the chopped nuts and figs during the last three minutes. Allow the dough to rest in the refrigerator for 12 hours.

Bring the ingredients for poaching the figs to a boil. Poach the figs for 1 minute and allow the fruit to cool in the liquid.

Sauté the cuttings, cloves and shallot for the sauce in 0.35 oz (10 g) olive oil and deglaze with one of the portions of red port. Allow to reduce, add the other portion of red port and reduce again. Add both types of stock and reduce to 0.8 cups (2 dl). Strain the sauce and mount with 0.7 oz (20 g) chilled pats of butter.

Wrap the piece of goose liver in the green cabbage leaves. Roll out the brioche dough to a thickness of 0.2 inches (0.5 cm). Place the goose liver on a slice of dough, coat the sides of the dough with beaten egg yolk and cover with a larger slice of dough. Firmly press the top slice to the bottom slice, and coat with beaten egg white.

Leave the brioche for 1 hour to adjust to room temperature and bake in a warm oven at 356°F (180°C) for 12 minutes. Leave the brioche to stand for 4 minutes and cut into 4 or 8 equal slices. Arrange the figs and dress the sauce in front of it.

Bordeaux, Saint-Julien or Saint-Estèphe

INGREDIENTS FOR 4

For the sauce:
1.2 cups (3 dl) veal stock (see base recipes)
3 oz (85 g) poultry stock (see base recipes)
2 x 1.75 oz (50 g) red port
2 cloves
2.1 oz (60 g) chopped shallot
3.15 oz (90 g) chicken cuttings
⟨⟩

1 piece goose liver of 12.25 oz (350 g)
4 fresh figs
⟨⟩

For poaching:
1.2 cups (3 dl) red wine
0.6 cups (1.5 dl) red port
0.6 cups (1.5) dl crème de cassis
1.2 cups (3 dl) water
1 cinnamon stick
3.5 oz (100 g) sugar
6 blanched green cabbage leaves
⟨⟩

For the brioche:
10.5 oz (300 g) all purpose flour
0.35 oz (10 g) fresh yeast
0.7 oz (20 g) sugar
0.35 oz (10 g) salt
4 eggs and 7 oz (200 g) butter
⟨⟩

For the filling:
0.88 oz (25 g) hazelnuts
0.88 oz (25 g) pecan nuts
0.88 oz (25 g) almonds
0.88 oz (25 g) pine nuts
1.4 oz (40 g) dried figs

Polenta filled with goose liver and truffle, with a creamy black salsify sauce

INGREDIENTS FOR 4

For the polenta:

1.1 lb (500 g) water

4.2 oz (120 g) polenta

0.1 oz (3 g) salt

1.75 oz (50 g) soft butter

1.93 oz (55 g) grated parmesan cheese

❦

For the sauce:

4.4 oz (125 g) peeled black salsify or oyster plant

(7 oz or 200 g including the peel)

0.35 oz (10 g) shallot

3.85 oz (110 g) poultry stock (see base recipes)

and 3.5 oz (100 g) cream

❦

2 whole black salsifies (oyster plants)

Peanut oil for deep-frying

24 large spinach leaves

4 goose liver medallions of 0.8 inches (2 cm)

thick and 1.2 inches (3 cm) in diameter

4 slices truffle

Add the polenta to the water and bring to a boil while stirring constantly. Cook the polenta over low heat for 25 minutes, while stirring every 2 minutes. Once cooked, season the polenta with soft butter, grated cheese and salt.

Wash the spinach leaves and blanch briefly.

Brown the goose liver medallions in a hot pan with 0.35 oz (10 g) peanut oil, and allow the medallions to cool. Once cooled, wrap the medallions in the spinach leaves.

Peel and chop the salsify for the sauce, sauté with the shallot in 0.35 oz (10 g) of olive oil, add the poultry stock and cream and allow it to cook until done. Blend the sauce and strain.

Wash the salsify to be used for deep-frying well, and cut one salsify into very thin circles without peeling. Wash the other salsify well cut into thin slices, without peeling. Heat the oil to 320ºF (160ºC) and deep-fry the circles and the slices until they turn golden yellow and crisp.

Fill half of a 2.4 inch (6 cm) ring with the warm polenta, place slices of truffle on the goose liver medallion and press into the center of the warm polenta. Fill up with polenta. Ensure that you have equal amounts of polenta on all sides of the medallion. Allow the polenta to cool in a refrigerator.

Remove the ring from the polenta and color a golden yellow on all sides in 0.35 oz (10 g) of hot oil. Heat the polenta for 6 minutes more in an oven at 338ºF (170ºC). Slice the polenta down the middle and arrange the pieces on top of each other, a long strip of deep-fried salsify next to it, decorate with a few pieces of deep-fried salsify and some circles in the sauce.

 Solid white wine from Piedmont, Chardonnay Ca' del Bosco

Everything appears to happen without any effort: Edwin Kats instructs his cooks in a gentle voice ("in the beginning we had to get used to that modest tone", says one member of the team), he casts his eyes over the hissing and steaming dishes and taps two tablespoons while 'turning quenelles'. That is what it is called in the trade. In the home kitchen, we would simply say he is modeling neat little ovals, and that from five different types of pureed vegetable. They are arranged in a circle on the plate, like splashes of paint on a palette, with a vegetarian club sandwich in the center. I can see it becoming an artistic whole, with much attention paid to details like the order of the colors of the quenelles. Obviously, a sandwich at *La Rive* cannot simply be a doubled-over piece of bread: the leavened bread comes from the internationally renowned Parisian baker Polaîne, and the sandwich is made with creamy hand-whipped mayonnaise, home-dried tomatoes and a quail's egg, sunny side up. Second chef Dennis bakes them four at a time, striving for ultimate perfection, partly for the picture photographer Bart van Leuven will soon be taking of the dish. From the quartet of quail's eggs the chefs unanimously pick the best: the yolk exactly centered and a rind of lacy egg white neatly removed with a cutter. Edwin shoves the plate under lamps, turns it by a degree or two, Bart clicks, and a moment later I am allowed to taste the quenelles: soft, with an unbelievably intense taste.

Vegetables

Nearly every self-respecting chef will work with asparagus and spinach in spring, tomatoes and sweet peppers in summer, and celeriac and Savoy cabbage in autumn and winter. But Kats's vegetable selection is more interesting than that: varieties that many will categorize as 'forgotten heroes' proudly adorn the plates here, like the salsify or oyster plant, turnips and even rutabaga, often disparagingly viewed as animal feed. The supply of fresh greens is up to delicious standard with dandelion, beet leaf and summer purslane. The chef uses the Jerusalem artichoke – that whimsically shaped North American tuber with a taste of nut, celery and artichoke – and parsnip: a white root with intense flavor and aroma, once more commonly eaten than any potato. A special place is reserved not only for the often ignored legumes (always double shelled, even the *petits pois...*), but also for cardoon, the excellent ancient thistle (related to the artichoke) from which the blanched stems are eaten. The artichoke, for that matter, is also used in a unique way at *La Rive:* served as carpaccio with a vegetable tartlet, one part of the bottom gets a glaze of vegetable bouillon while the other is destined for deep-frying, with a golden yellow and crisp effect. The age-old commanding instruction to "eat your vegetables!" will never be considered punishment within the walls of the Amstel: they are a treat.

Carpaccio of artichoke bottom with a tartlet of eggplant, zucchini, tomato, sweet pepper and olives, with flat-leaved parsley vinaigrette

INGREDIENTS FOR 4

4 large artichokes
Peanut oil for deep frying
0.4 cups (1 dl) vegetable bouillon
(see base recipes)
~

For the vegetable tartlet:
1 eggplant
1 green zucchini
1 yellow zucchini
2 red sweet peppers
2 yellow sweet peppers
20 black olives
6 home-dried tomatoes (see base recipes)
~
2 cups (0.5 liter) peanut oil to sauté the peppers
~
8 tablespoons of vinaigrette (see base recipes)
1 teaspoon parsley chlorophyll (see base recipes)
4 sprigs chervil

Peal the sweet peppers and remove the stems and seeds. Sauté the peppers in the peanut oil over a low heat (176°F or 80°C). If soft after 1 hour, remove the sweet peppers from the oil and grill on one side, cut 12 circles and chop the remaining flesh.

Halve the eggplant lengthwise, score and fill the cuts with salt, pepper, bay leaf, thyme, rosemary, garlic and olive oil. Roll the eggplant in aluminum foil and roast in the oven for 40 minutes at 284°F (140°C). Allow the eggplant to cool slightly, and peel. Chop the flesh and leave to drain on paper towel.

Peel the artichokes and cut the bottoms into thin slices, leaving 'closed' and 'open' slices (with and without holes). Glaze the 'closed' slices with the vegetable bouillon, and deep-fry the 'open' slices at 150°C until they are golden yellow and crispy.

Cut the zucchini into *batonettes* (see base techniques) and blanch.

Cut the olives into 24 rings; chop the rest and mix with the chopped sweet pepper.

Arrange the zucchini in cutters, and assemble the tartlet with tomato, eggplant and sweet pepper, continuing until it is filled up. Round off the tartlet with slices of sweet pepper, olive and a sprig of chervil.

Mix the chlorophyll with the vinaigrette à la minute and pour around the zucchini. Finish the dish with the slices of deep-fried artichoke.

Savennières (Chenin Blanc)
Sauvignon Blanc from Alto Adige or Neusiedlersee

Palette of vegetable puree with a club sandwich of goat's milk cheese, tomato and quail's eggs

INGREDIENTS FOR 4

5.25 oz (150 g) bunched carrots *brunoise*
5.25 oz (150 g) beet *brunoise*
5.25 oz (150 g) artichoke bottom *brunoise*
5.25 oz (150 g) fennel *brunoise*
5.25 oz (150 g) celeriac *brunoise*
12 quail's eggs
6 slices leavened bread
8 halves home-dried tomatoes (see base recipes)
8 slices of goat's cheese
24 sprigs rocket
2.6 oz (75 g) mayonnaise (see base recipes)

Glaze the vegetables individually with 0.07 oz (2 g) of salt and 4 tablespoons of vegetable bouillon (see base recipes). While still warm, blend the vegetables in a blender and strain. Allow the various kinds of puree to drain on a cloth until they reach the right consistency (reasonably thick).

Toast the leavened bread and cut circles of 2 inches (5 cm) each. Carefully open the 12 quail's eggs with a sharp pointed knife and fry over low heat in a non-stick pan. Ensure that 4 eggs do not break (sunny side up). Bake the other 8 on both sides. Cut the 4 most presentable eggs into neat circles (remove the ragged egg white rinds).

Spread the leavened bread with mayonnaise. Construct the sandwich with a slice of tomato, rocket, slice of goat's cheese, egg (fried on both sides), toast, more tomato, rocket, goat's cheese, egg (also fried on both sides), toast, and (finally) the neatly cut circle of quail's egg.

Form *quenelles* with the vegetable puree and arrange in a fan (or 'palette') on the plate; the club sandwich is placed in the center.

Dry white Vouvray
Lugana
White wine from the Savoy

Gratinated tarte tatin of candied chicory with chanterelles, beet leaves and thyme oil

INGREDIENTS FOR 4

14 heads chicory
4 round slices of puff pastry, baked

⤳

To gratinée:
5 egg yolks
3.5 oz (100 g) gastric (see base recipes)
2 tablespoons extra virgin olive oil
1.75 oz (50 g) whipped cream

⤳

32 presentable, small chanterelles
24 beet leaves
8 tablespoons thyme oil (see base recipes)
12 spring onions
2 fennel roots
1.4 oz (40 g) of poultry stock (see base recipes)

Scrape clean the chanterelle stems, slice off the tips and rinse in lukewarm water. Leave to dry on a cloth.

Cut the fennel roots in half and braise with 0.35 oz (10 g) of butter and 1.4 oz (40 g) of poultry stock. When they're done, cut the roots in small sections, put on olive oil and grill them.

Clean the chicory heads and stew with 1.4 oz (40 g) of butter and 0.8 cups (2 dl) vegetable bouillon. Once the heads are done, remove them from the non-stick pan and halve lengthwise. Brown chicory with 1.75 oz (50 g) butter and 0.7 oz (20 g) sugar in a non-stick pan until golden yellow, caramelizing the sugar in the process.

Pick the beet leaves and wash well.

Whisk the egg yolks and gastric *au bain-marie* until the mixture binds. Fix with the olive oil, allow it to cool, and mix with the half whipped cream.

Cut the spring onions into long *chinoise*, blanch and stew with a small pat of butter.

Arrange the candied heads of chicory on the pastry and evenly cover with the sauce. Gratinée the chicory in a hot oven.

Sauté the chanterelles in a small amount of oil over a low heat. Add a small pat of butter, salt and pepper towards the end. Allow the chanterelles to drain on a kitchen towel.

Place the *tarte tatin* at the center of the plate, surrounded by the chanterelles, segments of fennel, spring onion and beet leaves. Lastly, spoon some thyme oil over the vegetables.

Californian Sauvignon Blanc
New Zealand Riesling

Lukewarm salad of autumn vegetables with fritters of frogs' legs, with creamy parsley and garlic dressing

INGREDIENTS FOR 4

Wash the truffle potatoes well and boil in the skin, allow them to cool slightly and peel. Cut the potatoes into 20 slices.

Remove the leaves from the sprouts and blanch. Do the same with the celeriac, Swedish turnip, salsify, bunched carrot and Savoy cabbage.

Clean the artichokes and cut into thin slices. Glaze with 3.5 oz (100 g) vegetable bouillon.

Heat the vegetables in the stock and mix with the salads. Season to taste with salt and pepper.

Clean the frogs' legs in such a way that 1 bone is exposed, cover with fritter batter and deep-fry for 2 minutes in oil at 356°F (180°C) until a golden yellow.

Mix the dressing with the garlic puree and the parsley chlorophyll.

Arrange the salad on a plate, spoon over some dressing and place the fritters on top of the salad.

For the vegetable salad:
20 *chinoise* of celeriac
20 Swedish turnip bulbs
20 strips salsify
20 strips bunched carrot
1.4 oz (40 g) Savoy cabbage *bâtonettes*
12 small artichokes
20 slices truffle potato
16 sprouts

Mesclun (gourmet salad mix) of firm salad types:
cordifole, dandelion, beet leaves and *frisée*
(curly endive)

To heat the vegetables:
3.5 oz (100 g) poultry stock reduced to 0.88 oz
(25 g) and fixed with 2 tablespoons of extra
virgin olive oil

For the dressing:
3.5 oz (100 g) dressing (see base recipes)
0.35 oz (10 g) garlic puree (see base recipes)
1 tablespoon parsley chlorophyll
(see base recipes)

20 cleaned frogs' legs
7 oz (200 g) fritter batter (see base recipes)
Peanut oil for deep-frying

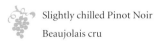
Slightly chilled Pinot Noir
Beaujolais cru

Crispy vegetable napoleons
and smoked salmon with coriander pesto

INGREDIENTS FOR 4

Deep-fry the eggplant, potato, artichoke, beet and celeriac individually at 302°F (160°C) until golden yellow and crisp. Salt the vegetables and store in a dry place.

Clean the leek and blanch the leaves, coat with olive oil and cut into strips of 7.9 inches (20 cm) long and 1.2 inches (3 cm) wide. Blanch the Savoy cabbage leaves and coat with olive oil. Also coat the raw zucchini slices with oil. Dry the Savoy cabbage and zucchini in an oven of 176°F (80°C) until crisp (leave the oven door ajar).

Wash the coriander well, dry and chop finely. Place in a blender with the garlic puree, almond and Parmesan. Blend the ingredients until they form a homogenous mass.

Stack the napoleon and place a slice of smoked salmon between the different types of vegetables. Lastly, position the beet and leek on top of the napoleon.

Arrange a few *quenelles* of coriander pesto and the whipped crème fraîche around the napoleon.

For the vegetable napoleons:
4 slices eggplant
4 slices zucchini
4 slices potato
4 Savoy cabbage leaves
4 strips leek
8 slices artichoke
12 slices beet
4 slices celeriac

Peanut oil for deep-frying
0.8 lb (360 g) thinly sliced smoked salmon

For the pesto:
1 bunch fresh coriander
1.75 oz (50 g) olive oil
0.7 oz (20 g) almond slivers
0.7 oz (20 g) grated Parmesan cheese
0.25 oz (7 g) garlic puree (see base recipes)

3.5 oz (100 g) whipped crème fraîche

Vernaccia di San Gimignano
Pinot Grigio from Collio and/or Southern Tirol
Roero Arneis from Piedmont, as young as possible

An affineur from the Alsace

An affineur
from the Alsace

He had a very humble start, this *affineur* Bernard Antony from the Alsace. Translated literally, he is a 'ripener' or a 'refiner': someone who ripens cheese to perfection under optimal conditions. Now the generally respected supplier of the most distinguished cheeses, he used to be the French equivalent of a grocery delivery boy. Antony gradually shifted his focus from home-delivered groceries to buying, caring for and selling cheese. Over time he managed to interest chefs in his products. Great chefs even, who came to rely on Antony (like Pierre Androuët, to whom Antony initially apprenticed himself to learn the basics of the trade).

After discussions with master Androuët, the *artisan-fromager* barred pasteurized cheeses from his collection and concentrated exclusively on traditional raw milk cheese. Since 1979 Antony has been the top player in the field of cheese, and has been able to hand-pick his clients, not only in France (where, among others, he supplies Alain Ducasse, Alain Passard, Pierre Gagnaire and Alain Senderens) but also internationally. Only if he likes the chef, and the chef's approach to cooking pleases him, will Antony accept him as a client. And only if the chef in question can show patience, as an appointment to meet and to taste some of the cheeses can usually not be made before three months have passed.

He had a very humble start, this *affineur* Bernard Antony from the Alsace. Translated literally, he is a 'ripener', or a 'refiner': someone who ripens cheese to perfection under optimal conditions. Now the generally respected supplier of the most distinguished cheeses, he used to be the French equivalent of a grocery delivery boy. Antony gradually shifted his focus from home-delivered groceries to buying, caring for and selling cheese. Over time he managed to interest chefs in his products. Great chefs even, who came to rely on Antony (like Pierre Androuët, to whom Antony initially apprenticed himself to learn the basics of the trade).

After discussions with master Androuët, the artisan-*fromager* barred pasteurized cheeses from his collection and concentrated exclusively on traditional raw milk cheese. Since 1979 Antony has been the top player in the field of cheese, and has been able to hand-pick his clients, not only in France (where, among others, he supplies Alain Ducasse, Alain Passard, Pierre Gagnaire and Alain Senderens) but also internationally. Only if he likes the chef, and the chef's approach to cooking pleases him, will Antony accept him as a client. And only if the chef in question can show patience, as an appointment to meet and to taste some of the cheeses can usually not be made before three months have passed.

La Rive, too, can revel in Antony's cheeses, which acts as the finale to a rural French dinner with their potent nature. Manager Christian Beek and chef Edwin Kats visited the great cheese supplier where he lives and works in Vieux-Ferrette, a town of 600 souls in the hills of the Alsace, close to the Swiss border. They were impressed. Kats: "I find it impressive to see how this man has worked to rise from humble grocer to his current status. But even more important: to see with how much passion he runs his business. It's modest in size, though – I expected significant areas filled with cheese, but his turnover is so high that they only spend a short time lying in one of his five cellars before being delivered to clients; optimally ripened, of course. From this dot on the map all the delicious Beauforts, Saint-Nectaires, Munsters, Livarots and other types go to restaurants on five continents, from the United States and Singapore to Amsterdam, to us."

Bernard Antony, balding, with his friendly bespectacled face, is generally regarded as the best affineur in the world. "I knew absolutely nothing about marketing", he once stated flatly, but he understood his trade and that proved to be more than enough. Antony understood that cheeses have seasons, and that during the ripening process each type called for a specific temperature and degree of humidity. If he trusts the taste of a chef, he would even ripen cheese to the chef's exact specifications. Cheeses redolent of the soil, their base milk originated from cows, sheep and goats grazing on fragrant grass, flowers and herbs. These elements, like the micro-organisms in the air, food and water, are taken up by the milk as natural flavoring agents. Edwin Kats: "He knows them all, the cheese farmers he buys his products from. They are often very small, and located all over France, but he knows exactly which cheese farmer hidden somewhere in Burgundy can deliver the best *chèvre*, or which farmer in the Aurillac region can offer him the right *cantal*. A chef can depend 100% on Antony for providing pure, gently aged cheese of an exceptionally high standard."

Favoured cheeses of Edwin Kats

Banon à la feuille
A Provençal mountain cheese made from goats' milk. After two weeks of *affinage* (or refining), the cheese is dunked in eau-de-vie and wrapped in a chestnut leaf.

Brie de Meaux (AOC)
This cows' milk cheese has a white velvety crust, which will acquire a red coloring on the top and sides as the cheese ages. It smells slightly moldy and has sweet, smoky flavor and a dense taste.

Brillat-Savarin
Enriched with cream and made with cows' milk from Normandy, this cheese was named after the famous 18th-century culinary author Brillat-Savarin.

Brin d'amour
Made from fresh goats' milk, this cheese from Corsica has a crust covered with summer savory and rosemary.

Chaource (AOC)
Creamy, lightly salted cheese produced from fresh cows' milk from the Champagne-Ardennes and Burgundy regions. The cheese has a soft interior paste with a rind of white mold.

Comté (AOC)
Together with Beaufort, this cheese made from fresh cows' milk from the Jura Mountains is one of the most popular cheeses in France. 530 liters of milk is required to produce a single cheese.

Fourme d'Ambert (AOC)
A mild, slightly salty blue mold cheese made from milk from the Auvergne.

Livarot (AOC)
This cows' milk cheese from Basse-Normandy was nicknamed 'Colonel', as the bands of paper with which it is bound resemble the stripes of a colonel.

Pierre-Robert
A mild cows' milk cheese enriched with cream from Seine-et-Marne, with a soft paste and a white mold crust.

Reblochon de Savoie (AOC)
A fresh, young and soft mountain cheese from the Savoy made of fresh, full milk.

Reypenaer VSOP
From the Dutch Woerden, this two year-old cows' milk cheese has a hard, crumbly structure and a salty, full taste.

Sainte-Maure de Touraine (AOC)
A goats' milk cheese covered in salted charcoal ash, with a walnut flavor.

Saint-Nectaire (AOC)
A typical Auvergne cheese produced from the milk of Salers cows, with the taste of salt, walnut, copper and herbs.

Vacherin Mont d'Or (AOC)
A winter cheese made of fresh cows' milk from the Massif du Mont d'Or in Franche-Comté, sold in a wooden box in which ripening continues.

Valençay
A goats' milk cheese from the province of Berry in central France. According to legend, the Valençay cheese originally had a perfect pyramid shape. Returning from his disastrous campaign in Egypt, Napoleon stopped by the Valençay castle, saw the cheeses, and in a blind rage used his sword to slice the tops off all the pyramids.

It was practically the first statement Edwin Kats made when I spoke to him about this book: "...and then there's a chapter dedicated to variety meats. They have such an excellent taste and structure; they should be on every menu – and in this book. Of course I understand that the subject of 'offal' can be a sensitive one in the Netherlands sometimes, but you are denying yourself something extremely tasty if you don't eat it. We can learn a lot from the Belgians and the French here. And besides, we prepare it in a reasonably subtle way in our kitchen, such as in a salad with goose liver, truffle and pig's feet. Obviously, you won't get the whole foot on your plate, just neat, cooked meat, dusted with bread crumbs and then grilled."

Variety meats

Like Kats, the famous culinary author M.F.K. Fischer loved variety meats. The American writer discovered this delicacy in rural France, and she is frank about the impression *tête de veau* made on her on first eating it. Not because of the calf's head, but because it was halved. One ear, half a forehead and one eye (although frivolously shut in mid-wink). And, of course, half a tongue, in Fischer's words: "lolling stiffly from the neat half-mouth". Nevertheless, Fischer ate it, and right she was. At any rate, those who say they do not like variety meats forget smoked sausage on kale or croquettes on the beach. And isn't every liverwurst, larded or not, a shining example of variety meat?

Loving liverwurst paves the way to sweetbreads, or *tripes*, eaten on holidays in France. The visitor to Scotland cannot really claim to have been there without tasting *haggis* (made from sheep's intestines). The same goes for Greek Easter celebrations that can only really be celebrated with a bowl of soup, ladled from a tureen in which a floating goat's head is quite normal. Robust, classic dishes. Just as classic but combined in surprising ways and presented in a modern fashion, are variety meats at *La Rive*, where something as delicious as 'glazed calf's sweetbread with onion compote, dried tomato and moussaka of calf's tongue with eggplant' can be found on the menu, accompanied by *beurre blanc* with olives...

What makes variety meats unique, as Edwin Kats rightly remarks, is the structure and wide variety of tastes, something the Japanese sum up as *umami*: the so-called 'fifth taste', which appears to combine aspects of the other four and can be summed up as 'the taste of meat'. In addition, the possible combinations with other types of meat are seemingly endless. Kats demonstrates this in both the separate chapter on goose liver – variety meat *par excellence* – and in his apparent difficulty in limiting the number of recipes for variety meats to only five...

Variety meats, in some cookbooks labeled as 'offal', come from an ancient tradition: for centuries these were the best you could serve someone, because of the uniqueness and the character. You do not deny yourself something as special as this for all the gold in the world.

Glazed calf's sweetbread with onion compote, dried tomato, moussaka of calf's tongue and eggplant, beurre blanc with olives

INGREDIENTS FOR 4

1.3 lb (600 g) heart sweetbread

7 oz (200 g) finely sliced onion rings

0.52 oz (15 g) dried tomato

0.4 cups (1 dl) poultry stock (see base recipes)

6 tablespoons gastric (see base recipes)

1.5 tablespoons cream

3.5 oz (100 g) chilled butter

Approximately 50 black olive rings

ورد

For the moussaka:

0.35 oz (10 g) sliced calf's tongue

1 peeled eggplant cut into thin slices

3 pomodori tomatoes cut into thin slices

2 large potatoes cut into thin slices

0.4 cups (1 dl) cream and 2 egg yolks

ورد

10.5 oz (300 g) veal stock (see base recipes),
mixed with 5.25 oz (150 g) poultry stock

Rinse and soak the sweetbreads in cold water for 36 hours, changing the water every 8 hours. Bring salted water to a boil and use to blanch the sweetbreads, then remove the skin and slice into 8 pieces of 2.45 oz (70 g).

Stew the onion rings to compote with the finely sliced tomato, poultry stock, salt and pepper.

Prepare the moussaka from the tomatoes, potatoes, eggplant and calf's tongue, layered in an ovenproof dish. Spread a small amount of a mixture of the cream and egg yolk between layers, sprinkled with some thyme and rosemary. Cover the moussaka and bake for 50 minutes at 356ºF (180ºC). Allow to cool, then pour, cut into long strips and heat in an oven at 320ºF (160ºC).

Sauté the sweetbreads in the peanut oil to a golden-yellow, then deglaze with a small amount of stock. Now baste with the stock, and keep adding small amounts of stock until the sweetbreads have a shiny glaze.

Mix the gastric with the cream and slowly add the pats of chilled butter. Add the olive rings last.

Arrange the onion compote in 2 cutters with a piece of sweetbread on each, and the moussaka and *beurre blanc* with olives in-between.

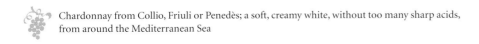

Chardonnay from Collio, Friuli or Penedès; a soft, creamy white, without too many sharp acids, from around the Mediterranean Sea

Salad of marinated potato, spinach and anise cap mushrooms with jellied calf's kidney, calf's tongue, and vinaigrette with calf's head and gherkin

INGREDIENTS FOR 4

4.2 oz (120 g) calf's kidney
0.8 cups (2 dl) poultry stock (see base recipes)
2 cups (5 dl) veal stock (see base recipes)
4.2 oz (120 g) thinly sliced, poached calf's liver
4.2 oz (120 g) thinly sliced, poached calf's tongue
28 slices grilled, marinated potato
12 tablespoons balsamic vinegar vinaigrette
(see base recipes)
40 young spinach leaves
24 anise cap mushrooms
0.88 oz (25 g) fine gherkin *brunoise*
1.75 oz (50 g) finely sliced calf's head
24 croutons
Assorted presentable salads (like mizuha,
cordifole, frisée (curly endive) and dandelion)

Rinse and soak 7 oz (200 g) calf's head overnight, then blanch and stew in the veal stock for 2½ hours at 311°F (155° C). Remove the calf's head from the stock, leave in the refrigerator to harden, and then cut into a fine *brunoise*.

Rinse and soak the calf's kidney overnight and poach in the poultry stock for 6 minutes.

Wash the potato well, and boil unpeeled in salted water until cooked. Peel the potatoes, cut into thin slices, cut into circles (1.5 inch – 4 cm) with a cookie cutter and grill. Marinate the slices for 4 hours in the balsamic vinegar vinaigrette (which can be used afterwards).

Wash the young spinach leaves and assorted types of salad well and dry.

Clean the anise cap mushrooms, wash carefully and cook over low heat without causing discoloring.

Build the salad with layers of the types of meat, spinach, assorted salads, anise caps and potato. Mix the gherkin and calf's head with the balsamic vinegar vinaigrette (left from marinating) and dress around the salad. Lastly add the croutons to the salad.

Lightly chilled Pinot Noir from the Alsace to wash and/or neutralize, or a white Graves to elevate

Clear lamb bouillon perfumed with smoked garlic and tarragon, glazed turnips and croquettes with variety meats of lamb

Heat a smoking pan with 0.35 oz (10 g) wood chips. Once the pan is smoking well, position the grill with 20 cloves of garlic and leave to smoke for 2 minutes. Bring lamb bones to a boil in salted water, skim the bouillon well, and add all other ingredients. Allow the bouillon to draw well over low heat for 8 hours, then strain and clear with minced meat, egg white, garlic and tarragon.

Rinse and soak the lamb kidneys in cold water for 36 hours. Put the brains away in wide water for 24 hours. Change the water every 8 hours. Use a sharp pointed knife to remove the membrane from the brain and put away in 1.2 cups (3 dl) milk for 24 hours. Then poach the brains in the bouillon for 6 minutes, the kidneys for 8 minutes.

Melt the butter for the *salpicon*, add the flour and dilute with the lamb bouillon. Add all the garnish and heat the *salpicon* thoroughly. Put everything in the refrigerator to set; then form small croquettes of 0.35 oz (10 g) each, bread them *à l'anglaise* and deep-fry in peanut oil at 356ºF (180ºC) until they turn golden-yellow.

Shape and glaze the spring turnips. Stew the turnips *à la minute* and mix with the freshly cut tarragon. Dress in the middle of a plate, cut the kidney into thin slices and arrange on the turnips, with a half brain on top. Pour the bouillon over and serve the croquettes separately.

INGREDIENTS FOR 4

For the bouillon:
4.4 lb (2 kg) sawn lamb bones
16 cups (4 liter) water
0.6 oz (17 g) sea salt
5.6 oz (160 g) peeled, canned tomatoes
0.53 oz (15 g) tomato puree
1.75 oz (50 g) leek
0.88 oz (25 g) celeriac
1.23 oz (35 g) celery stalk
2.1 oz (60 g) onion
1.05 oz (30 g) carrot
0.1 oz (3 g) peppercorns
0.07 oz (2 g) coriander seeds
1 bay leaf
½ sprig thyme
¼ sprig rosemary
10 smoked garlic cloves

To clear:
7 oz (200 g) lean lamb mince
10 smoked garlic cloves
1.75 oz (50 g) beaten egg white
0.7 oz (20 g) fresh tarragon

For the salpicon:
1.05 oz (30 g) flour
1.05 oz (30 g) butter
0.4 cups (1 dl) lamb bouillon
0.21 oz (6 g) garlic puree (see base recipes)
1.75 oz (50 g) *brunoise* of assorted mushrooms
0.04 oz (1 g) chopped parsley
4.2 oz (120 g) brunoise of lamb variety meats
(kidney, liver, heart, tongue and sweetbread).

60 shaped spring turnips
12 chopped tarragon leaves
2 lamb brains
2 lamb kidneys

Poached lamb shank with shoulder of lamb rillettes, baked lamb's brains, Reypenaer VSOP, Menton lemon and black olives

INGREDIENTS FOR 4

4 sawn lamb shanks
4 cups (1 liter) lamb stock (see base recipes)
4 lamb's brains

For the shoulder of lamb rillettes:
8.8 oz (250 g) lamb shoulder meat
4 cups (1 liter) melted goose fat
0.1 oz (3 g) coarse sea salt
0.04 oz (1 g) crushed peppercorn
1 bay leaf
1 sprig thyme
1 sprig rosemary
0.04 oz (1 g) coriander seeds

2.2 lb (1 kg) potatoes (Platat nr. 4)
peanut oil for deep-frying
48 French green beans (*haricots vert*)
48 slices Reypenaer VSOP

For the vinaigrette:
0.53 oz (15 g) 20 year-old balsamic vinegar
0.28 oz (8 g) 7 year-old balsamic vinegar
0.35 oz (10 g) lemon juice
(preferably from Menton, in France)
2.6 oz (75 g) olive oil
1.4 oz (40 g) extra virgin olive oil
2.8 oz (80 g) lamb stock
1.4 oz (40 g) reduced red wine
(2.8 oz or 80 g reduced to 1.4 oz or 40 g)
32 halves black olives
20 lemon zests

Marinate the shoulder of lamb in the herbs for 24 hours. Now cut the meat into rough pieces, and braise over low heat or in an oven at 248°F (120°C). This takes approximately 3 hours. Once the meat is done, remove from the pan and wrap in 1.05 oz (30 g) suet (kidney fat) and 0.7 oz (20 g) goose fat. Season the rillettes with salt and pepper.

Poach the shanks in the stock and spices for 150 minutes at 230°F (110°C).

Store the brains for 24 hours in ample water. Then remove the membrane around the brains with a paring knife, and store in 1.2 cups (3 dl) milk for 24 hours.

Shape the potatoes into round forms and turn into long spaghetti with a vegetable pasta maker. Rinse the spaghetti in cold water and blanch briefly, making sure they do not break.

Wrap a sheet of greaseproof paper around a 1.2 inch (3 cm) rvs ring and wind the spaghetti around it. Deep-fry everything at 320°F (160°C) until the tower turns a nice golden yellow. Fill the towers with the rillettes à la minute.

Clean the French green beans and blanch.

Slice the shanks into thin slices and arrange flat on a plate. Place the rillettes at the center with the tower, and arrange the French green beans, flakes of Reypenaer VSOP, the olives and the lemon zests around it.

Flour the brains à la minute and fry until crispy in 0.53 oz (50 g) olive oil. Arrange the brains on the potato tower. Distribute the olives around the dish and finish with a tablespoon of vinaigrette.

Lightly chilled, red Loire wine: Chinon, Saumur, Anjou: simple Cahors

"He's one of the few chefs at the very top of his profession who has saddle of wild boar on his menu – and who keeps it there, judging from the orders he places with me!" according to Pieter van Meel, game distributor. "And I take my hat off to him; properly preparing saddle of wild boar is an art, as the meat dries out very quickly. To me this means he knows his field extremely well."

The *La Rive* menu not only boasts wild boar from Veluwe, but also the signature dish 'Beemster saddle of hare', served with a *boudin* of own blood, or 'sweat of the hare' as it is called in hunting circles. The hunt has had its own language, laws and traditions for centuries, as expressed in classic dishes like 'partridge wrapped in bacon and covered with vine leaf'. Especially with game there are classics which chefs can really get into, whether prepared in the true classic way – after all, there is a reason why a dish becomes a classic – or prepared with a subtle modern or personal twist.

For Edwin Kats, to start with, the partridge should be a gray partridge; rarer than the somewhat bland tasting red bird (with white meat), the tastier and finer gray is held in high regard. Kats also fits the partridge with a jacket of bacon and vine leaf (sealing in moisture); but, with a nod to the plump bird, the blanched sprouts are also wrapped: they wear a robe of smoked bacon. The dish is rounded off with potato cakes, fragrant partridge *jus* and a dash of cognac, and finally mounted with goose liver butter. Simple *au fond*, but exactly as partridge should be, served by a chef who knows his classics.

Game

The partridge *(Perdrix perdrix)* originally came from Central Asia, but, subsequently, spread all over Europe. Today you will come across this small bird with his round body, known as 'perdiz' in Andalusia or *'patrys'* in Amsterdam. He only measures around a foot (30 cm) in length, but his compact form helps him carry a decent portion of meat: 12½ oz (350 gram) for a fully grown young bird.

Another bird from the east is the pheasant *(Phasanus colchicus)*, which hails from the Caucasus and regions around the Caspian Sea. According to mythology, Jason and the Argonauts (seeking the Golden Fleece) discovered this bird along with the precious Fleece in the city of Colchis. The city (now located in Georgia) can still be found in the bird's Latin name. Pheasant, called *'faizan'* in French, often adorns the tables of the nobility – for many centuries only they had the right to hunt these birds. For many people, pheasant hung by its feet for a few days (or even up to a few weeks) is still the only way to enjoy the meat. Instead of the old-fashioned hung pheasant, we might prefer the tender meat of a pheasant hen prepared in Kats's version today: poached in pheasant stock and adorned with a gratin of celeriac, porcini mushrooms and Parma ham. And, for lovers of furred game, there is a palette of deer. Beautiful game. And beautifully prepared.

Palette of Deer: saddle of deer medallion, stewed shank and poached leg, with Savoy cabbage and parsley

INGREDIENTS FOR 4

For the persillade:

0.35 oz (10 g) butter

1.23 oz (35 g) chopped parsley

0.53 oz (15 g) fine *brunoise* marrow

0.53 oz (15 g) fine *brunoise* mushrooms

0.35 oz (10 g) chopped shallot

15 chopped thyme leaves

5 chopped rosemary leaves

0.18 oz (5 g) bread crumbs

0.18 oz (5 g) garlic puree (see base recipes)

4 saddle of deer medallions of 1.75 oz (50 g)

4 deer shanks, sawn off at 2.75 inches (7 cm)

4 cups (1 liter) deer stock (see base recipes)

7 oz (200 g) leg of deer

0.2 cups (4 dl) deer stock (see base recipes)

7 oz (200 g) dried potato puree

1.4 oz (40 g) chilled pats of butter

4 appetizing Savoy cabbage leaves

5.6 oz (160 g) *bâtonettes* of Savoy cabbage

For the sauce:

1.4 oz (40 g) deer trimmings

0.53 oz (15 g) shallot

0.18 oz (5 g) butter

0.35 oz (10 g) red wine vinegar

1.4 oz (40 g) red wine

14 oz (400 g) deer stock

7 oz (200 g) porcini mushrooms (cèpes)

Blanch the 4 Savoy cabbage leaves, coat with oil and dry in an oven at 176ºF (80ºC) until they turn crisp. Keep the oven door ajar.

Brown the deer shanks and stew in the deer stock for 2.5 hours over low heat.

Remove the deer medallions from the refrigerator 2 hours before using, brown in 0.35 oz (10 g) olive oil and roast until done for 4 minutes in a preheated oven of 320ºF (160ºC).

Heat the potato puree with 1.05 oz (30 g) of milk and fix with the chilled butter.

Melt the butter and marrow for the *persillade*, and add the mushrooms, shallot, thyme, rosemary, garlic puree, bread crumbs and parsley. Blanch the Savoy cabbage *bâtonettes*, stew with a pat of butter and add the *persillade*.

Remove the leg of deer from the refrigerator 2 hours before using, heat the deer stock to 90ºC and poach the leg in the bouillon for 3 minutes.

Clean the porcini mushrooms, cut into small scallops, and sauté in 0.35 oz (10 g) butter over low heat.

For the sauce: melt the butter, brown the deer trimmings and chopped shallot; add wine vinegar and wine, allow to evaporate, and add the stock. Reduce the sauce over low heat and keep skimming. Once the sauce is reduced to 0.8 cups (2 dl), strain and fix *à la minute* with 0.7 oz (20 g) chilled pats of butter.

Arrange the potato puree on the plate, and place the shank on top. Cut the leg into slices, and arrange the porcini mushrooms on the slices. Decorate the cabbage with a medallion on top, stick a dried cabbage leaf in the potato puree and pour the sauce in-between.

 Red wine from the Côte de Nuits, for example a Morey-Saint-Denis

Poached pheasant breast with a gratin of celeriac, porcini mushrooms and Parma ham, with a creamy goose liver sauce

INGREDIENTS FOR 4

For the gratin:
0.77 lb (350 g) porcini mushrooms
1.2 cups (3 dl) cream and 3 egg yolks
8.8 oz (250 g) thin slices celeriac
5.25 oz (150 g) thinly sliced Parma ham

2 pheasant hens
4 cups (1 liter) pheasant stock (see base recipes)
5.6 oz (160 g) potato puree
Assorted types of firm salad: dandelion, *mizuha, cordifole, frisée* (curly endive) and beet leaves
8 tablespoons of balsamic vinegar
(see base recipes)

For the sauce:
3.5 oz (100 g) pheasant trimmings
0.7 oz (20 g) shallot
0.18 oz (5 g) goose fat
1.05 oz (30 g) white wine
7 oz (200 g) pheasant stock (see base recipes)
3.5 oz (100 g) cream
1.05 oz (30 g) goose liver butter (see base recipes)

12 spring turnip bulbs

Clean the porcini mushrooms and rinse in lukewarm water.

Mix the cream with the egg yolks; grease an ovenproof dish with melted butter and fill as follows: a layer of celeriac, some cream, slices of Parma ham, some more cream and thin slices of the porcini stems (the caps will be used for the salad). Repeat until all the ingredients have been used and 4 layers of each ingredient have been formed. Cover the dish and bake for 45 minutes in an oven at 338°F (170°C). Leave the gratin in a cool place for 6 hours and wait for it to set. Remove the gratin from the dish and cut into 4 long strips, squirt these with the potato puree and bake *à la minute* for 15 minutes in an oven heated to 338°F (170°C).

Remove the drumsticks from the pheasant and poach these in the pheasant stock over low heat for approximately 90 minutes. Now remove the bones from the drumsticks, trim the meat and slowly fry the skin side in 0.35 oz (10 g) goose fat, until the skin on the drumstick becomes crispy. Leave the breast on the carcass and poach this in the stock over low heat for approximately 22 minutes. Cut the breast from the carcass *à la minute* and carve in neat slices.

Brown the trimmings and shallot in the goose fat, add the wine, leave to reduce; add the stock and cream and reduce to 0.6 cups (1.5 dl). Strain the sauce and fix with the goose liver butter using a hand blender. Do not allow the sauce to boil after this.

Wash the various salads well and dry. Glaze the spring turnip bulbs. Wash the porcini caps and stew quickly with salt and 0.35 oz (10 g) olive oil. Toss the salad with the vinaigrette. Arrange the gratin on the plate, with the slices of pheasant in front and the sauce poured between gratin and pheasant. Serve the salad separately.

 Rich, ripe wine from the Libournais, a Château Lagrange from Pomerol, for example

Possibly a soft, soothing white Chardonnay, for example a Puligny Montrachet 'Les Pucelles', not too young

Dutch saddle of hare fillet
with chicory heads filled with apple compote,
blood sausage and a Calvados jus

INGREDIENTS FOR 4

2 Dutch saddles of hare
8 chicory heads
·꒳·

For the filling:
1 apple (Jonagold)
0.35 oz (10 g) butter
pinch of cinnamon
0.35 oz (10 g) sugar
·꒳·

8 thin slices Jabugo ham
12 slices blood sausage
(prepared with rabbit's blood, if you wish)
·꒳·

For the sauce:
1.4 oz (40 g) rabbit trimmings
0.53 oz (15 g) shallot
0.88 oz (25 g) apple (Jonagold)
0.35 oz (10 g) butter
1.05 oz (30 g) white wine
0.88 lb (400 g) rabbit stock (see base recipes)
0.35 oz (10 g) Calvados

Remove the fillets from the saddle with 5 small ribs still attached, clean these ribs, and remove the meat from the refrigerator 2 hours before using.

Pick the chicory heads and blanch the leaves. Peel the apple and slice into *brunoise*. Stew the apple with butter, sugar and cinnamon until cooked. Place the loose chicory leaves in the palm of your hand, arrange a small amount of apple compote on them, and close them to form a neat chicory head again. Roll this in a thin slice of ham. Slowly roast the head in 0.7 oz (20 g) of butter until warm.

For the sauce, brown the trimmings, shallot and apple in the butter, deglaze with wine, allow the liquid to reduce and add the stock. Reduce the liquid to 0.8 cups (2 dl) over low heat, strain and fix the sauce with 1.4 oz (40 g) of butter and a few drops of Calvados.

Cut the blood sausage into slices and sauté lightly in 0.7 oz (20 g) of butter until they have an appetizing color.

Brown the fillets in 0.7 oz (20 g) of butter and then bake in an oven at 320°F (160°C) for 4 minutes. Remove the meat from the oven, leave to rest in a warm spot for 6 minutes, and then fillet.

Arrange the 2 chicory heads with the slices of blood sausage to their left and the fillets in front. Evenly cover with the sauce.

Red wine from the Cahors
Argentine Malbec
A spicy, rich Saumur
Red Graves

Partridge prepared in vine leaf with sautéed sprouts in bacon, potato cakes and partridge jus

2 large (or 4 smaller) grey partridges

8 slices bacon for wrapping

16 presentable blanched vine leaves

48 sprouts

24 thin slices bacon

For the 12 potato cakes:

7 oz (200 g) dried potato puree

1.05 oz (30 g) egg yolk

0.18 oz (5 g) egg white

0.1 oz (3 g) potato starch

For the sauce:

1.75 oz (50 g) partridge trimmings

0.35 oz (10 g) cognac

2.8 oz (80 g) poultry stock (see base recipes)

1.05 oz (30 g) veal stock (see base recipes)

0.7 oz (20 g) pheasant stock (see base recipes)

1.05 oz (30 g) goose liver butter (see base recipes)

7 oz (200 g) assortment of various mushrooms (chanterelles, oyster mushrooms, porcini, shiitake, chestnut mushrooms, etc.)

Wash the potatoes (0.88 lb or 400 g, *bintjes*) well without peeling, place on a layer of course sea salt in the oven, and bake for 75 minutes at 320ºF (160ºC). Allow the potatoes to cool slightly and halve, remove the puree from the skin and push through a strainer while still warm. Mix the warm puree with the egg yolk, egg white and starch, roll into balls of 0.88 oz (25 g) each and sauté these in oil over low heat until an even golden-yellow color.

Clean the partridge (or ask the butcher to do this), cover with the slices of bacon, wrap in the vine leaves and keep these in place with thin kitchen string. Take the partridges out of the refrigerator 2 hours before preparation. First sauté the partridge over low heat for 6 minutes on each drumstick in 0.35 oz (10 g) of goose fat, then brown all around, and roast for 6 minutes in a preheated oven at 356ºF (180ºC). Remove the partridge from the oven and leave to rest in a warm area for 12 minutes. Remove the vine leaves and bacon, and slice off the drumsticks and breast.

The assortment of mushrooms will be served underneath the partridge, and should be prepared as follows: clean, rinse in lukewarm water, dry on a towel and sauté in 0.7 oz (20 g) of butter.

Blanch the sprouts. Roll each sprout in a thin slice of smoked bacon and carefully sauté in 0.7 oz (20 g) of oil until golden-yellow.

Brown the trimmings for the sauce in 0.35 oz (10 g) of goose fat, deglaze with the cognac, add the stock and allow everything to draw for 6 minutes. Strain the sauce and fix with the goose liver butter using a hand blender.

Arrange the partridge on top of the mushrooms with the potato cakes and the sprouts around it. Pour the sauce over the partridge.

 A sweet bird with the softest, finest red
Côte de Beaune: Volnay

Possibly a white wine: the rarest Alsatian Riesling

The patisserie is one of the most delightful places in the *La Rive* kitchens. From early morning it smells of freshly baked bread (the baker comes in at six), soon followed by sweet hints of ice cream, syrup and fresh fruit. Here, right behind the cold kitchen, the pastry chefs are baking almond *tuiles*, raising soufflés and constructing meringue baskets. These feathery products will become the building blocks for the fruit desserts Edwin Kats likes to prepare. For this book he selected five fruit desserts, based on apple, strawberries, grapefruit, raspberries and peach.

Fruit

We see apples as the fruit of Paradise, but other cultures regard figs, quinces and pomegranates as originating from the Garden of Eden. Once, in the wild, the apple was not much more than a dressed core. Until the Romans came: they gave the layer of flesh between the core and the peel some body, and managed to cultivate at least 30 different types. Today, we are still picking the fruits of their labor, sinking our teeth into or preparing it as Kats demonstrates, by filling an oven-baked apple with almond paste and giving it a boost with cloves, aged Madeira and orange zabaglione. On top of it all rests a *tuile*, like a roof tile.

Since time immemorial strawberries have come from the three B's: Bergen op Zoom and Beverwijk in the Netherlands, and Beervelde in Belgium: well-known cultivation areas for full baskets. They originated from the wild strawberries that, despite their small size, have an enormous concentration of flavor and taste. Already in the 16th century epicureans wrote of the joy of strawberries with cream, a classic combination loved from center court at Wimbledon to the heart of *La Rive*, where creamy honey mousse accompanies an ice and jelly of 'regular' and wild strawberries.

Apart from the apple, another fruit is often linked to Paradise: the Latin name for grapefruit is *Citrus Paradisi*. The 'forbidden fruit' was discovered on Barbados around 1750. We know the largest member of the citrus family as 'grapefruit' not because it looks like a grape, but because they grow in *grappes*, or bunches. We find the fruit quartered at *La Rive*, marinated in white port and served with cream in which only the most flavorful vanilla features: grown on the island of Ile de Bourbon, now known as Réunion.

Two more dishes adorn the dessert menu: the supreme Persian fruit, the peach (from the Latin *persicum*, meaning 'Persian fruit'), baked and basted with orange caramel, with a *quenelle* of cool vanilla ice cream; and the classic French toast, with a tartar of fresh fruit, with mango and papaya. Completely in style this is accompanied by curds of the softest, most tender summer fruit known in the Low Lands: raspberries.

Grapefruit marinated in white port
with a cream of balsamic vinegar and bourbon vanilla

INGREDIENTS FOR 4

For the meringue baskets, heat the egg white with the 1.75 oz (50 g) icing sugar until it reaches body temperature, then whisk with a food processor until cooled down. Once properly cooled, fold the remaining 0.88 oz (25 g) of sugar into the mixture. Squeeze a few dots on greaseproof paper, squirt the baskets around them and dry in an oven of 158°F (70°C) (this will take approximately 12 hours). When finished, use a sharp pointed knife to remove the dots and scrape clean the insides of the baskets.

Reduce the balsamic vinegar and mix with the crème fraîche, vanilla marrow, sugar and mascarpone. Leave the crème in the refrigerator for 1 hour to thicken. Reduce the white port by half with the sugar and ginger, leave to cool and allow the grapefruit segments to marinate in this for 12 hours.

Fill the baskets with crème. Arrange the grapefruit segments around this, and sprinkle with some zest and 3 tablespoons of marinating liquid. Garnish the baskets with the almonds, prune compote and gold leaf.

For the cream:
7 oz (200 g) crème fraîche
1.75 oz (50 g) mascarpone cheese
1.23 oz (35 g) sugar
the marrow of 1 vanilla pod
2 tablespoons of reduced balsamic vinegar
(8 tablespoons reduced to 2)

40 grapefruit segments
4.4 oz (125 g) white port
1.4 oz (40 g) sugar
0.7 oz (20 g) fresh ginger
24 grapefruit zests

For the meringue baskets:
1.75 oz (50 g) egg white
1.75 oz (50 g) icing sugar
0.88 oz (25 g) icing sugar

8 roasted almonds
4 tufts of prune compote
4 bits of gold leaf (varak)

Recioto di Soave
Sweet Orvieto wine

Coupe filled with strawberry ice, honey mousse and wild strawberries

INGREDIENTS FOR 4

For the honey mousse:
12.25 oz (350 g) cream
2.8 oz (80 g) honey
2 gelatin sheets
(equal to 2 teaspoons gelatin powder)
∞

For the ice:
8.8 oz (250 g) strawberry pulp
(left over from the jelly)
0.88 oz (25 g) honey
0.88 oz (25 g) sugar
∞

For the strawberry jelly:
8.8 oz (250 g) strawberries
0.88 oz (25 g) sugar
2 gelatin sheets
80 presentable wild strawberries

Mix the strawberries and sugar for the jelly, and store *au bain-marie* in a bowl covered with plastic for 2 hours. Retain the liquid, and use 0.07 oz (2 g) gelatin for every 3.5 oz (100 g) liquid.

Mix the pulp left over from the jelly with the sugar, and leave in a bowl in the freezer. Drag a whisk through the ice every 30 minutes to form attractive flakes of ice.

For the mousse, heat the honey slightly and use to dissolve the gelatin. Whip the cream to the consistency of yoghurt and mix with the cool honey. Leave the mousse to set in the refrigerator for 4 hours.

Fill the chilled coupes with the strawberry ice, add a layer of honey mousse, and arrange the wild strawberries on top. Finish with the jelly.

Chenin Blanc from the Côteaux du Layon
Bonnezeaux
Sweet Vouvray

Oven-baked peach with nuts, an orange-caramel sauce and vanilla ice cream

Mix all ingredients for the cookies and leave to rise overnight. Allow the dough to reach room temperature and roll out to 0.1 inch (2 mm) on grease-proof paper. Slice into wedges and cut a circle on the bottom side; bake for 10 minutes at 392°F (200°C).

Allow the sugar for the sauce to caramelize over low heat; add the butter, lemon juice, orange juice and nuts. Pour the liquid with the nuts over the peaches. Place the dish in the oven and bake the peaches at 392°F (200°C) for 10 minutes, basting the peaches with the liquid once every minute. Add the orange segments for the last 2 minutes.

Boil the milk and cream; beat the sugar and marrow from the vanilla pods. Add the warm cream and milk to the sugar mass and mix well. Leave the mixture to stand in the refrigerator overnight, and turn to ice cream in the machine the next day.

Arrange the warm peaches on a plate, evenly cover with the warm sauce, and arrange the cookies behind each peach with a *quenelle* of vanilla ice cream.

INGREDIENTS FOR 4

4 peeled peaches

For the orange-caramel sauce:
3.5 oz (100 g) sugar
5.25 oz (150 g) butter
juice of ¼ lemon
3.5 oz (100 g) orange juice
2.6 oz (75 g) chopped almond
2.1 oz (60 g) chopped hazelnut
1.75 oz (50 g) pistachio kernels
2.6 oz (75 g) sliced orange sections

For the vanilla ice cream:
2 vanilla pods
4.7 oz (135 g) sugar
8.2 oz (235 g) milk
8.2 oz (235 g) cream
3.5 oz (100 g) egg yolk

For the cookies:
2.6 oz (75 g) sugar
4.4 oz (125 g) flour
2.6 oz (75 g) butter
0.35 oz (10 g) egg
a pinch of finely ground cinnamon

Beerenauslese from the Neusiedlersee in Austria and/or Germany
Fresh sweet with acids: Vin de Constance from South Africa

French toast baked in spices,
with a tartar of fresh fruit and raspberry curd

Peel the fruit and dice into a neat brunoise.

Melt the honey and butter for the tuiles, add the other ingredients, squirt a line on grease-proof paper and finally bake the *tuiles* for 6 minutes at 302°F (150°C). Cover the brioche buns with the French toast batter and fry until golden brown in 0.7 oz (20 g) peanut oil. Cut out the bread in circles and make little tarts with the fruit.

Allow the yoghurt to rest on a cloth for 12 hours, and then mix with the raspberry *coulis* and sugar. Allow this to set in the refrigerator for 4 hours.

Place a *quenelle* of curd on each tartlet, with a *tuile* on top and surround with some raspberry coulis.

INGREDIENTS FOR 4

24 brioche buns

0.79 lb (360 g) tartar of fresh fruit: mango, kiwi, papaya, pineapple, strawberries and melon

·×·

For the French toast batter:

3.5 oz (100 g) cream

3.5 oz (100 g) milk

3 eggs

2.1 oz (60 g) icing sugar

the marrow of 1 vanilla pod

·×·

For the tuiles:

2.1 oz (60 g) butter

2.8 oz (80 g) honey

4 oz (115 g) sugar

4.2 oz (120 g) flour

3 oz (85 g) egg white

·×·

2.1 oz (60 g) raspberry *coulis*

·×·

For the raspberry curd:

1.1 lb (500 g) yoghurt

3.5 oz (100 g) raspberry *coulis*

4.4 oz (125 g) sugar

0.7 oz (20 g) peanut oil

 Sauternes and/or a similar wine from the Bordeaux region

Baked apple with clove and aged Madeira, served with orange zabaglione

INGREDIENTS FOR 4

Peel and core the apples, stuff with the almond paste, pierce with a metal cocktail pick and roll in the sugar and clove mix.

Melt the sugar for the caramel. Once melted, carefully add the Madeira wine.

Pour the caramel over the apples, and bake them at 392°F (200°C) for 20 minutes, basting with the caramel every 3 minutes.

Melt the honey and butter for the *tuiles*, and then add the rest of the ingredients. Cut a cross from a mould of 16 by 16 cm and push the dough into this.

Bake the tuiles at 302°F (150°C) for 6 minutes, then immediately place each tuile over an orange to obtain the correct shape.

Mix all ingredients for the zabaglione and whisk *au bain-marie*. Place the apples at the centre of the plate, pour over the zabaglione and place the tuile over this.

4 firm, presentable apples
(such as Golden Delicious or Red "Boskoop")

For the Madeira caramel:
3.5 oz (100 g) brown castor sugar
3.5 oz (100 g) white castor sugar
5.25 oz (150 g) Madeira wine

3.5 oz (100 g) almond paste
10.5 oz (300 g) sugar mixed with 0.07 oz (2 g) ground clove

For the orange zabaglione:
3.5 oz (100 g) egg yolk
2.1 oz (60 g) orange juice
2.28 oz (65 g) white wine
1.75 oz (50 g) sugar
1.23 oz (35 g) Grand Marnier
the juice of ½ lemon

For the tuiles:
2.1 oz (60 g) butter
2.8 oz (80 g) honey
4 oz (115 g) sugar
4.2 oz (120 g) flour
3 oz (85 g) egg white

Sweet Madeira (Bual)
Vin Santo
French Muscat

Base Techniques

Arrange
To position ingredients on a plate in a visually pleasing way

Baste
To repeatedly sprinkle or cover a dish with a fatty liquid, such as butter

Bâtonettes
Ingredients cut into strips of equal size (usually 1.6 inches/4 cm long and 0.2 inches/5 mm wide)

Binding
Tying together pieces of poultry or meat with kitchen string in order to preserve its shape

Blanch
Cooking ingredients in salted water for a short time, then (importantly) quickly cooling in cold water, possibly with ice cubes

Blend
To blend ingredients into a fine sauce or substance

Breading anglaise
Coating an ingredient, first with flour, then with beaten egg white, and finally with bread crumbs or breading flour

Brunoise
Ingredients cut into cubes of equal size (usually 0.2 inches/5 mm)

Caramelize
a. Carefully heating sugar to form a caramel
b. Adding a small amount of sugar during preparation and stewing slowly

Chinoise
Vegetables cut into diamonds

Clarify
To turn a bouillon into a clear liquid using beaten egg white and minced fish, meat or vegetables

Fillet
To remove the bones from fish or meat

Garnish
Adding a finishing touch to a dish

Glaze
Preparing ingredients with stock or butter to obtain a glossy finish

Gratinée
To form a crust on a dish

Grind
To reduce ingredients to fine bits in a blender or food processor

Infusion
Herbs steeped in liquid over low heat, resulting in a pleasant, soft taste

Julienne
Ingredients cut into equal strips (usually 1.6 inches/4 cm long and 0.04 inches/1 mm wide)

Marinate
Coating ingredients with a liquid or with dry herbs to tenderize or give a specific taste

Mount
A sauce is mounted by adding pats of chilled butter or oil to a warm sauce or coulis

Plisser
To peel or skin ingredients (e.g. tomatoes) by poaching them for seconds only and plunging them quickly into iced water

Poach
Cooking products in a liquid at just under boiling point

Pouring
Pouring sauces or other liquids neatly (and sometimes partly) on food

Quenelle
A dish with a soft consistency shaped into an oval using a cold or warm spoon

Reduce
To boil a liquid uncovered over medium heat to concentrate the flavor

Rounding
Term originating from French: cutting vegetables into a specific elegant form, using a paring knife

Sauté
Frying in butter or oil for a short time without browning, which releases the flavor

Shred
Slice into very thin pieces

Skim
Removing unwanted froth from a sauce or bouillon with a ladle during preparation

Stew
Slowly cooking over low heat in a covered dish

Strain
Passing a liquid through a sieve or a cloth

Strips
Long, thin slices of (sometimes oven dried) vegetables (usually 3.9 inches/10 cm long and 0.4 inches/1 cm wide)

Base Recipes

The recipes seldom mention salt and pepper. For us it is evident to season all dishes to taste with salt and pepper.

When using an oven, a few points are extremely important:
- it should always be preheated to the correct temperature
- time is given as a guideline only, and the size of the oven plays an important role: the smaller the oven, the faster heat is lost when it is opened
- it makes a big difference whether it is a gas, convection or combination oven.

Always use the same measuring cup, spoon or scale when measuring ingredients.

Be sure to heat plates for dishes which are to be served warm; for example, by placing them in an oven.

Balsamic vinegar vinaigrette

0.4 cups (1 dl) balsamic vinegar – 0.8 cups (2 dl) regular olive oil – 0.4 cups (1 dl) extra virgin olive oil – 0.4 cups (1 dl) peanut oil – 0.8 cups (2 dl) reduced veal stock

Mix all the ingredients. The vinaigrette is ready for use immediately.

Basic dressing

0.88 oz (25 g) egg yolk – 0.2 cups (0.5 dl) walnut oil – 1.6 cups (4 dl) peanut oil – 0.35 oz (10 g) Dijon mustard – 0.2 cups (0.5 dl) organic vinegar – 0.2 cups (0.5 dl) water – 0.53 oz (15 g) icing sugar – 0.07 oz (2 g) salt – 0.02 oz (0.5 g) pepper

Beat the egg yolk with the mustard, vinegar, icing sugar, pepper, salt and water, and add the oil a few drops at a time. The dressing should form a proper homogenous mass.

Court-bouillon

10 cups (2.5 liters) water – 0.4 cups (1 dl) white wine – 2 cloves – 5.25 oz (150 g) carrot – 2 star anise – 2.6 oz (75 g) fennel – 2.6 oz (75 g) celery stalk – 1 bay leaf – a pinch of cayenne pepper – the zest of 1 orange – ½ fresh pimento

Bring all ingredients to a boil and subsequently use to boil or poach the desired ingredients (fish, lobster, etc.).

Fines herbes

0.35 oz (10 g) flat-leaved parsley – 0.21 oz (6 g) chervil – 0.14 oz (4 g) tarragon – 0.14 oz (4 g) coriander – 0.28 oz (8 g) chives

Cut the chives into very small rings using a sharp knife. Wash the remaining herbs well and chop.

Fish fumet

1.3 lb (600 g) fish bones – 1.75 oz (50 g) onion – 0.7 oz (20 g) shallot – 0.7 oz (20 g) white of leek – 0.7 oz (20 g) mushrooms – 0.35 oz (10 g) parsley – 2 garlic cloves – 1.23 oz (35 g) white wine – 0.7 oz (20 g) Noilly Prat – 1 sprig of thyme – 1 bay leaf – 0.25 oz (7 g) salt – 12 peppercorns – 15 coriander seeds – 2.4 cups (6 dl) water

Clean the fish bones and wash well. Bring to a boil with the water and salt. Add all other ingredients and allow the stock to draw over low heat for 20 minutes. Strain the fumet.

Fritter batter

5.25 oz (150 g) all purpose flour – 1 egg yolk – 0.45 oz (13 g) fresh yeast – 0.3 cups (0.75 dl) milk – 0.5 cups (1.25 dl) beer

Dissolve the yeast in the lukewarm milk, stir all ingredients to a smooth batter, and allow it to rise in a warm place for 1 hour. Store the batter in the refrigerator and mix à la minute with 1 part beaten egg white (a ratio of 1:1).

Garlic puree

2 garlic bulbs – 0.8 cups (2 dl) milk

Blanch the garlic cloves in water twice, and then boil in milk for 10 minutes until done. Peel the cloves and force through a strainer.

Gastric

7 oz (200 g) shallots – 4 garlic cloves – 0.14 oz (4 g) peppercorns – 0.07 oz (2 g) coriander seeds – ½ bay leaf – ½ sprig thyme – 1.6 cups (4 dl) white wine – 0.2 cups (0.5 dl) tarragon vinegar – 0.3 cups (0.75 dl) Noilly Prat – 1.5 cups (4 dl) water

Fry the shallots in 0.35 oz (10 g) of oil, add the remaining ingredients and allow to reduce over low heat to 8.8 oz (250 g).

ॐ

Goose liver butter

3.5 oz (100 g) soft butter – 3.5 oz (100 g) soft goose liver

Mix the butter and goose liver using a food processor or blender, then form small blobs using a pastry bag.

ॐ

Herbal chlorophyll

3.5 oz (100 g) fresh green herbs (parsley, celery leaves, basil, chervil, coriander, tarragon) – 1.75 oz (50 g) spinach

Blend the herbs and spinach with 1.75 oz (50 g) water for 10 minutes. Squeeze the pulp well in a cloth, and be sure to save the liquid! Bring the liquid to a boil, stirring constantly. At 203ºF (95ºC) the chlorophyll will separate from the moisture – now add 10 ice cubes and quickly cool the liquid. Pour back into a cloth – the puree remaining in the cloth is the chlorophyll.

ॐ

Herbal oil

3.5 oz (100 g) different green herbs – 0.4 cups (1 dl) arachid oil

Blanch the green herbs, blend with the oil and leave the mixture for 10 minutes, then strain.

ॐ

Home-dried tomato

6 tomatoes – 0.35 oz (10 g) olive oil – 1 minced garlic clove – 0.7 oz (20 g) shallot – 1 sprig of thyme – 1 sprig of rosemary – 1 bay leaf

Peel the tomato (see base techniques), quarter and remove the pulp; season with salt, pepper, olive oil, sliced shallot, the clove of garlic, thyme and rosemary. Place the sections in an ovenproof dish and dry in the oven at 194ºF (90ºC) for 60 minutes, with the door partially open: moisture from the tomatoes should be allowed to evaporate, in order to concentrate the flavor.

Lobster coulis

1.1 lb (500 g) lobster carcasses – 0.7 oz (20 g) carrots – 0.7 oz (20 g) celery stalk – 0.7 oz (20 g) white of leek – 0.7 oz (20 g) fennel – 0.7 oz (20 g) onion – 0.53 oz (15 g) shallot – 1 garlic clove – 1.4 oz (40 g) tomato puree – 6.13 oz (175 g) peeled, canned tomatoes – ½ bay leaf – ½ sprig thyme – 0.88 oz (25 g) cognac – 2.1 oz (60 g) white wine – 4 basil leaves – 4 cups (1 liter) water

Method: Bruise the carcasses in a food processor and fry in 0.35 oz (10 g) of oil, add the vegetables and brown with the carcasses, and finally add the tomato puree and peeled tomatoes and brown for a further 30 seconds. Deglaze with the wine and cognac, and add the water and all remaining ingredients. Allow everything to draw for 20 minutes; add the basil during the last 5 minutes. Strain the liquid and allow the coulis to reduce to taste.

ॐ

Mayonnaise

0.42 oz (12 g) sherry vinegar – 0.14 oz (4 g) Dijon mustard – 0.1 oz (3 g) salt – 1.75 oz (50 g) egg yolk – 2 cups (0.5 liter) grape seed oil – 0.7 oz (20 g) water (allow all ingredients to reach room temperature before using)

Beat the yolk with the mustard, vinegar, salt and water. Add the oil a few drops at a time. The mixture should become a proper homogenous mass.

ॐ

Oxtail bouillon

2.2 lb (1 kg) sawn oxtail – 3.85 oz (110 g) peeled, canned tomatoes – 0.35 oz (10 g) tomato puree – 0.35 oz (10 g) salt – 0.07 oz (2 g) peppercorns – 0.88 oz (25 g) white of leek – 0.53 oz (15 g) celeriac – 0.7 oz (20 g) celery stalk – 1.05 oz (30 g) onion – 0.53 oz (15 g) carrot – ½ sprig thyme – ½ sprig rosemary – 0.04 oz (1 g) coriander seeds – 1 garlic clove – 8 cups (2 liters) water

Brown the oxtail in the oven at 320ºF (160ºC) for 20 minutes. Bring the pieces to a boil with the water and salt. Skim well, and add the vegetables and remaining ingredients. Allow the bouillon to draw over low heat for 6 hours, strain and clarify with 3.5 oz (100 g) clear meat (lean ground beef mixed with egg white).

ॐ

Pheasant stock

17.5 oz (500 g) carcasses – 2 cups (0.5 l) veal stock – 3.2 cups (0.8 l) poultry stock

Boil the carcasses up with the stock, skim well and allow to draw for 60 minutes, then strain.

Pigeon, rabbit and duck stock

1.1 lb (500 g) carcasses of the respective animals – 2 cups (0.5 liter) brown veal stock – 4 cups (1 liter) poultry stock

Brown the carcasses in an oven at 320ºF (160ºC) for 15 minutes. Add the cold stock to the carcasses and bring to a boil, then allow it to draw over low heat for 1.5 hours. Strain the stock.

ᘓ

Poultry stock

1.4 lb (650 g) chicken carcasses, wings or necks – 15 coriander seeds – 0.04 oz (1 g) peppercorns – ½ sprig rosemary – 1 sprig thyme – 1 bay leaf – 1 garlic clove – 0.35 oz (10 g) shallot – 0.7 oz (20 g) onion – 0.35 oz (10 g) white of leek – 0.35 oz (10 g) celery stalk – 0.18 oz (5 g) celeriac – 8 cups (2 liters) water

Bring water to a boil with salt and carcasses, and skim well. Add all other ingredients and allow the stock to draw for 2 hours over low heat, then strain.

ᘓ

Shrimp oil

17.5 oz (500 g) shrimp carcasses – 0.7 oz (20 g) carrot – 0.7 oz (20 g) celery stalk – 20 white of leek – 0.7 oz (20 g) fennel – 0.7 oz (20 g) onion – 0.53 oz (15 g) shallot – 1 garlic clove – 1.4 oz (40 g) tomato puree – 6.13 oz (175 g) canned, peeled tomatoes – ½ bay leaf – ½ sprig of thyme – 0.88 oz (25 g) cognac – 2.1 oz (60 g) white wine – 5 basil leaves – 4 cups (1 liter) grape seed oil

Bruise the carcasses in a food processor and brown in 0.35 oz (10 g) of oil, add the vegetables and fry together, then add the tomato puree and peeled tomatoes and fry for a further 30 seconds. Deglaze with the wine and cognac, and add the remaining ingredients and oil. Allow everything to draw for 20 minutes at 158ºF (70ºC). Add the basil during the last 5 minutes, and then strain the oil.

ᘓ

Stock of deer and hare

2.2 lb (1 kg) carcasses – 4 cups (1 l) veal stock – 2.4 cups (6 dl) water

Brown the carcasses in an oven of 356 ºF (160 ºC) for 20 minutes. Add the cold veal stock and the water. Bring to a boil, allow the stock to draw over low heat for 1.5 hours, then strain.

ᘓ

Thyme oil

0.7 oz (20 g) thyme – 0.14 oz (4 g) parsley – 0.4 cups (1 dl) peanut oil

Blanch the thyme and parsley, blend with the oil and leave the mixture for 10 minutes, then strain.

Vegetable bouillon

2.1 oz (60 g) onion – 3.85 oz (110 g) carrot – 1.05 oz (30 g) white of leek – 2 garlic cloves – 1 beefsteak tomato – 0.35 oz (10 g) celery stalk – 1.93 oz (55 g) fennel – 0.7 oz (20 g) shallot – 15 peppercorns – 0.18 oz (5 g) coriander seeds – 1 blade of mace – 0.2 cups (0.5 dl) white wine – 0.2 cups (0.5 dl) Noilly Prat – 4 tarragon leaves – 1 parsley stalk – 3 basil leaves – 6 coriander leaves – 0.21 oz (6 g) salt – 4 cups (1 liter) water

Bring all ingredients to a boil and allow to draw (or steep like tea) for 1.5 hours at 167ºF (75ºC), then strain the bouillon.

ᘓ

Veal stock

2.2 lb (1 kg) veal bones – 2.1 oz (60 g) carrot – 1.4 oz (40 g) onion – 1.58 oz (45 g) celery stalk – 1.05 oz (30 g) celeriac – 2.1 oz (60 g) white of leek – 2 garlic cloves – 0.42 oz (12 g) salt – 30 coriander seeds – 35 peppercorns – ½ sprig rosemary – 1 sprig thyme – 1 bay leaf – 3.85 oz (110 g) peeled, canned tomatoes – 1.93 oz (55 g) tomato puree – 0.6 cups (1.5 dl) red wine – 8 cups (2 liters) water

Method: Fry the vegetables (including the garlic) in 0.35 oz (10 g) of oil, add the tomato puree and peeled tomatoes and fry together for 30 seconds. First add the wine and remaining ingredients (excluding the water and bones), only then add the water and the bones. Bring everything to a boil, and skim well. Allow the stock to draw over low heat for 6 hours, then strain.

ᘓ

Vinaigrette

0.1 oz (3 g) Dijon mustard – 0.2 cups (0.5 dl) champagne vinegar – 0.3 cups (0.75 dl) extra virgin olive oil – 0.4 cups (1 dl) olive oil – ½ garlic clove – 1 basil leaf – 1 sprig of thyme – 1 small sprig of rosemary

Mix all the ingredients and allow it to stand in the refrigerator for 24 hours. Strain the vinaigrette before using.

ᘓ

White veal stock

2.2 lb (1 kg) veal bones – 1.58 oz (45 g) onion – 1.93 oz (55 g) celery stalk – 1.23 oz (35 g) celeriac – 2.45 oz (70 g) white of leek – 1 garlic clove – 0.6 cups (1.5 dl) white wine – 0.5 oz (14 g) salt – ½ sprig rosemary – ½ sprig thyme – ½ bay leaf – 0.07 oz (2 g) peppercorns – 0.07 oz (2 g) coriander seeds – 8 cups (2 liters) water

Bring water to a boil with the salt and bones, and skim well. Add all other ingredients and allow the stock to draw for 6 hours over low heat, then strain.

Register

Truffles

24   Cassoulet of frogs' legs, white beans and beet with a hint of lime and black winter truffle shavings

27   Braised cheeks and feet of free-range pigs with Savoy cabbage, creamed shallot, Jabugo ham and white truffle

28   Roast rib of Limousin calf with a soufflé of fennel and truffle, and pink peppercorn and Parmesan sauce

30   Warm ballotine of Dutch rabbit with truffle, small shallots and green asparagus

33   Creamy truffle risotto with Parmesan cheese, a baked free-range egg and fresh, shaved white truffle

Asparagus

36   Crispy roasted asparagus with a salad of spring vegetables, vinaigrette of Vin Santo vinegar and truffle

38   Lukewarm asparagus spaghetti with grilled, lightly smoked East Scheldt lobster, garlic fritters and lemon thyme

40   Asparagus tips in cream with poached free-range egg, morels and broad beans

43   'Pot au feu' of glazed veal shank with asparagus and spring vegetables

Potatoes

57   Cannelloni of potato and smoked salmon with cucumber and Osetra caviar

58   La Ratte potato mousse with tartar of oysters and herbs, potato tuile, slices of smoked salmon and green asparagus

60   Croquettes of salted cod, potato and Bélon oysters, creamy sauce of young leeks and Osetra caviar

63   Creamy potato soup and nutmeg with goose liver ravioli and celery

64   Turbot and truffle wrapped in potato spaghetti with stewed Swiss chard and light veal gravy

Crustaceans and shellfish

68   Dry, baked coquilles St. Jacques with a fresh goat's cheese and basil mousse, and sweet-and-sour pumpkin and onion compote

70   Salad of North Sea crab prepared with green herbs, served with lemon gingersnaps and a spicy gazpacho

73   Grilled coquilles St. Jacques with cauliflower au gratin, tartar of oysters and green herbs, and potato sauce

74   Poached fillet of sole with lobster tortellini, corn and grilled sweet pepper tartlet, and beurre blanc with lime and thyme

76   Slices of smoked salmon with a salad of lobster, North Sea crab, shrimp and fine vegetables

Poultry

80   Poached 'Anjou Royal' pigeon, corn crêpes filled with goose liver and creamy black pepper sauce

82   Sautéed Miéral duck with all trimmings, sweet-and-sour spring turnip and purslane

85   Roasted Miéral guinea fowl with baked salsify, Vin Santo sauce and nutmeg

86   Roasted Dutch 'Blauwpoot' chicken with Jabugo ham, sautéed chicory and a creamy oloroso sherry sauce

Goose liver

102   Terrine of Jabugo ham, goose liver and stew steak with oxtail jelly and Szechuan pepper

105   Goose liver gratinée with duxelles of mushrooms, cubes of calf's tongue and escargots, with aged Madeira sauce

106   Salad of pig's feet, goose liver and truffle, with a dressing of petits pois and celery

109   Goose liver baked in a fig and nut brioche with a red port and clove sauce

110   Polenta filled with goose liver and truffle, with a creamy black salsify sauce

Vegetables

114   Carpaccio of artichoke bottom with a tartlet of eggplant, zucchini, tomato, sweet pepper and olives, with flat-leaved parsley vinaigrette

117   Palette of vegetable puree with a club sandwich of goat's milk cheese, tomato and quail's eggs

118   Gratinated tarte tatin of candied chicory with chanterelles, beet leaves and thyme oil

120   Lukewarm salad of autumn vegetables with fritters of frogs' legs, with creamy parsley and garlic dressing

123   Crispy vegetable napoleons and smoked salmon with coriander pesto

Variety meats

136   Glazed calf's sweetbread with onion compote, dried tomato, moussaka of calf's tongue and eggplant, beurre blanc with olives

139   Salad of marinated potato, spinach and anise cap mushrooms with jellied calf's kidney, calf's tongue, and vinaigrette with calf's head and gherkin

140   Clear lamb bouillon perfumed with smoked garlic and tarragon, glazed turnips and croquettes with variety meats of lamb

143   Poached lamb shank with shoulder of lamb rillettes, baked lamb's brains, Reypenaer VSOP, Menton lemon and black olives

Game

147   Palette of Deer: saddle of deer medallion, stewed shank and poached leg, with Savoy cabbage and parsley

148   Poached pheasant breast with a gratin of celeriac, porcini mushrooms and Parma ham, with a creamy goose liver sauce

150   Dutch saddle of hare fillet with chicory heads filled with apple compote, blood sausage and a Calvados jus

153   Partridge prepared in vine leaf with sautéed sprouts in bacon, potato cakes and partridge jus

Fruit

156   Grapefruit marinated in white port with a cream of balsamic vinegar and bourbon vanilla

158   Coupe filled with strawberry ice, honey mousse and wild strawberries

160   Oven-baked peach with nuts, an orange-caramel sauce and vanilla ice cream

163   French toast baked in spices, with a tartar of fresh fruit and raspberry curd

164   Baked apple with clove and aged Madeira, served with orange zabaglione

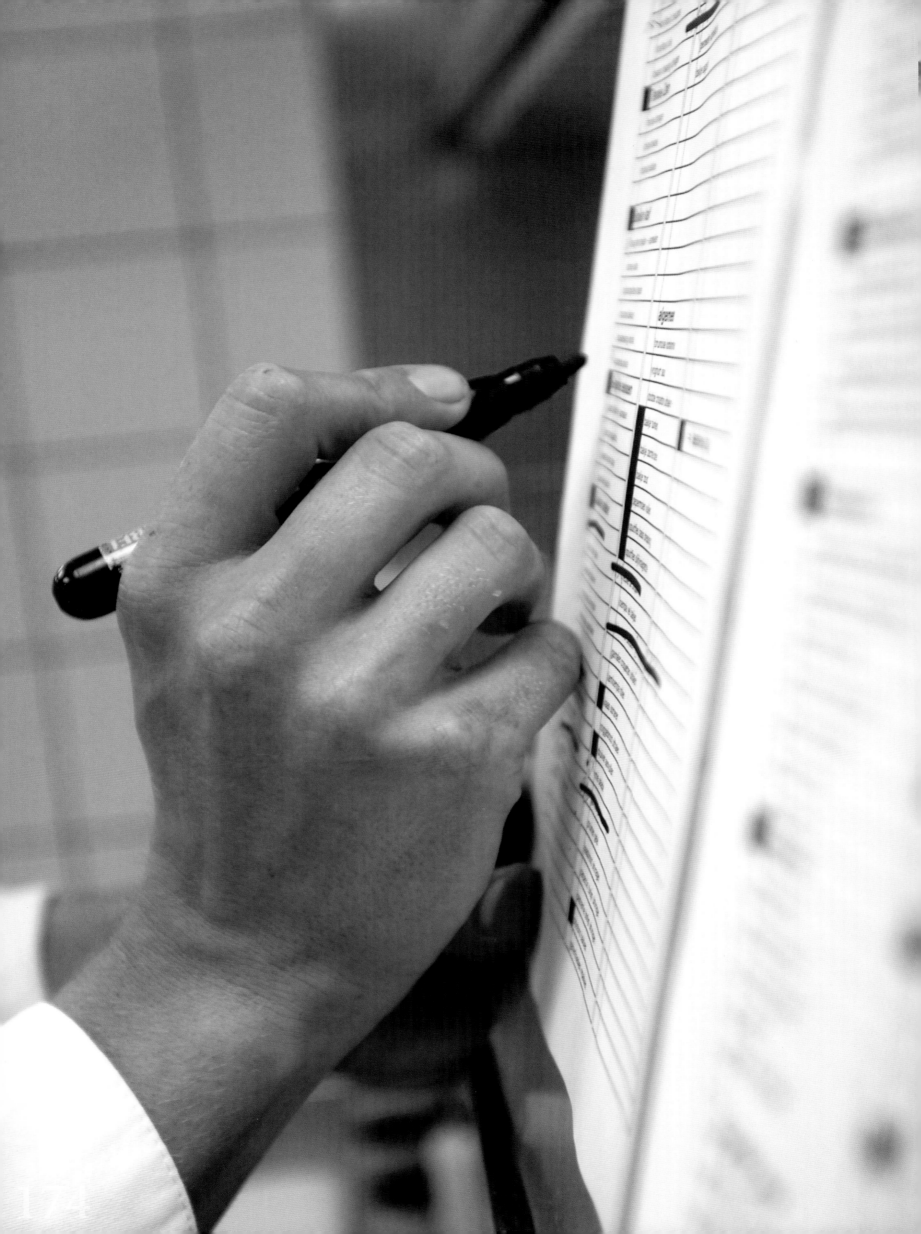

Colophon

Authors
Edwin Kats
Alma Huisken

Photography
Bart Van Leuven

Concept
Jaak Van Damme

Co-ordination
Philippe Degryse

Final editing
Femke De Lameillieure

Layout and Photogravure
Graphic Group Van Damme, Oostkamp

Printed by
Graphic Group Van Damme, Oostkamp

Binding
Scheerders-Van Kerchove, Sint-Niklaas

Published by
Stichting Kunstboek
Legeweg 165
B-8020 Oostkamp
Tel.: + 32 (0) 50 46 19 10
Fax: + 32 (0) 50 46 19 18
E-mail: stichting_kunstboek@ggvd.com
www.stichtingkunstboek.com

ISBN: 90-5856-097-X
NUR: 441
D/2003/6407/9

INTERCONTINENTAL.
AMSTEL
A M S T E R D A M

Restaurant La Rive
Amstel Inter-Continental
Prof. Tulpplein 1
NL-1018 GX Amsterdam
tel.: + 31 (0) 20 622 60 60
fax: + 31 (0) 20 622 58 08